# Democracy and National Pluralism

For moral and practical reasons, in recent years there has been a growing interest in issues related to the recognition of different national groups within the same democracy. Belgium, Canada, Spain and the UK are examples of plurinational democracies which are currently reviewing the way in which their minority nations, such as the Flemish, Québécois, Catalans and the Scottish are – and should be – treated in liberal and democratic terms.

Renowned international researchers in this book address the major questions of the conceptual and practical revision of plurinational liberal democracies at the beginning of the twenty-first century: political equality and citizenship; the cultural neutrality of the state; nationalism in the era of globalisation; the collective dimension of individual rights; and the institutional accommodation of different national collectivities in the public sphere of democratic politics, and of recent supra-state structures such as the European Union.

*Democracy and National Pluralism* will be a much needed resource for researchers in politics, international relations, political philosophy and public policy who are examining the contemporary challenges facing democracies and their relationship with the diverse national groups that coexist in their territories.

**Ferran Requejo** is Professor of Political Science at Pompeu Fabra University, Barcelona. In 1997 he was awarded the Rudolf Wildenmann Prize (ECPR). He is the co-editor of *European Citizenship, Multiculturalism and the State*.

# Routledge Innovations in Political Theory

# Democracy and National Pluralism

Edited by Ferran Requejo

London and New York

First published 2001
by Routledge
11 New Fetter Lane, London EC4P 4EE

Simultaneously published in the USA and Canada
by Routledge
29 West 35th Street, New York, NY 10001

*Routledge is an imprint of the Taylor & Francis Group*

Typeset in Sabon by BC Typesetting, Bristol
Printed and bound in Great Britain by
TJ International Ltd, Padstow, Cornwall

*British Library Cataloguing in Publication Data*
A catalogue record for this book is available from the British Library

*Library of Congress Cataloging in Publication Data*
Democracy and national pluralism / edited by Ferran Requejo.
    p.   cm. – (Routledge innovations in political theory; 8)
    Includes bibliographical references and index.
    ISBN 0-415-25577-5 (alk. paper)
    1. Democracy. 2. Pluralism (Social sciences). 3. Minorities–Civil
rights. 4. Minorities–Political activity. I. Requejo Coll, Ferran.
II. Series.

JC423 .D439795 2001
323.1–dc21                                           2001019455

ISBN 0-415-25577-5

To all our PhD students

# Contents

# Contributors

**Ferran Requejo** is Professor of Political Science at Universitat Pompeu Fabra, Barcelona, Catalonia, Spain.

**Will Kymlicka** is Professor of Philosophy at Queen's University, Kingston, Ontario, Canada.

**Michael Keating** is Professor of Political Science at the University of Aberdeen, Scotland, United Kingdom.

**Enric Fossas** is Associate Professor of Constitutional Law at Universitat Autònoma de Barcelona, Catalonia, Spain.

**Wayne Norman** holds the Chair in Business Ethics in the Centre for Applied Ethics at the University of British Columbia, Vancouver, Canada.

**Carlos Closa** is Associate Professor of Political Science at Universidad de Zaragoza, Spain.

**Ricard Zapata** is Associate Professor of Political Science at Universitat Pompeu Fabra, Barcelona, Catalonia, Spain.

# 1 Introduction

## 'It is so very late that we may call it early by and by'

*Ferran Requejo*

In a nocturnal scene, on seeing dawn's light entering the room where he is standing, one of the characters in Shakespeare's *Romeo and Juliet* exclaims: 'It is so very late that we may call it early by and by.'[1] Something similar could be said of the current situation of liberal democracies. Their theoretical health and undeniable practical success over the past two centuries do not hide, however, some of the conceptual and institutional shortcomings they display when faced with the 'new dawn' that some aspects of politics are experiencing at the beginning of the twenty-first century.

Democratic liberalism has established itself as the most desirable, from a theoretical perspective, and the most stable, from a practical perspective, of all contemporary political traditions. It has a diverse and plural history that has been written by thinkers of acknowledged intellectual prestige such as Locke, Madison, Jefferson, Kant, Toqueville, Mill, Weber, Berlin and Rawls. Its values and legitimising principles have shown themselves to be more suitable for practical application than those of alternative political theories. Furthermore, democratic liberalism is a practical and constitutional tradition that has no rivals among present-day political systems. It has been so successful that issues such as the protection of rights and freedoms, the existence of competitive elections and of an effective form of political pluralism, the implementation of the principles of constitutionality and legality, the separation and the division of powers or the articulation of a market economy with a degree of public interventionism have become generally accepted 'meta-values' in Western societies.

However, this intellectual and constitutional solidity and the absence of rival political systems does not mean that liberal democracies can consider themselves entirely 'just' systems that have no drawbacks or features that work against emancipation; or that they are somewhere at 'the end of history'. Nor does it mean that it is easy to find new

normative and institutional solutions from its legitimising and organisational principles when it comes up against new political challenges.
This is true, for example, when it is forced to deal with such phenomena
as globalisation, cultural pluralism or new kinds of international relations. When faced with these phenomena, the language, the institutions
and even the usual interpretation of fundamental liberal and democratic values – liberty, equality, pluralism or dignity – require a revision
of the theory and, above all, a series of practical and constitutional
reforms that will bring about a moral improvement and a better
adaptation to the new economic, political, cultural and technological
conditions that prevail at the beginning of the twenty-first century.

   One of the two main elements of this book is a revision of the theory
of democratic liberalism from the perspective of one of the main
phenomena of cultural pluralism: the national pluralism that exists in
some democracies – plurinational democracies. This work contributes
to the debate that has emerged during the 1990s concerning the rights
of cultural minorities and liberal democracy. This is a debate that
explodes the myth that empirical democracies are neutral in relation
to cultural pluralism. Nowadays it is difficult to argue that the recognition of the cultural rights of minorities within a democracy is inherently
discriminatory or arbitrary. There are fewer and fewer liberal theorists
who still maintain that liberal-democratic institutions are neutral when
dealing with cultural issues, and there are also fewer who oppose the
regulation of certain cultural rights, including the rights of national
minorities. This discussion has also helped to reveal the intellectual
difficulties that traditional democratic liberalism displays when it has
to deal with the cultural pluralism of contemporary societies. These
difficulties are related, at least partly, with two theoretical attitudes
of traditional liberalism. First, there is the tendency to use a number
of extremely abstract legitimising categories – individual rights, citizenship, equality, and so on – which often leads to a homogeneous interpretation of these categories, which in turn makes it more difficult to
deal with their internal pluralities. Second, the selection of a number
of 'research questions' that usually causes traditional democratic liberalism to take for granted and refuse to revise the linguistic, historical
and political culture of majority 'national' groups. Cultural identities
constitute, along with interests and values, a third element of democratic legitimacy, as well as an element of individual dignity. This is
an aspect that has been largely marginalised by traditional liberal-
democratic theories.

   We are becoming increasingly aware of the hegemonic cultural
particularisms that hide behind the ostensibly neutral and universal

concepts and discourse of liberal-democratic theories. We are becoming increasingly aware of the power relations that operate in the cultural sphere, in addition to those related to social class and gender, to cite but two. It would appear that classical liberal agnosticism practised with regard to religion cannot be extrapolated to issues such as linguistic policies, school curricula or the 'national' self-perception of democratic collectives. This is and will increasingly be related to the regulation of citizenship in democracies which, as we enter a new century, shows all the signs of being characterised by increasing internal cultural pluralism and by a growing process of globalisation.

The other main theme in this volume is the recognition and practical accommodation of national pluralism in democratic polities. Of all the challenges faced by present-day democracies, those related to national pluralism have been, and continue to be, problematical from both a conceptual and an institutional standpoint. This is the case when the legitimacy of any given state is called into question or when, in more moderate terms, distinct national collectives express a wish to be recognised as such constitutionally and to enjoy their own form of national self-government within the democratic polity. This is the case of existing democracies such as Belgium, Canada, Spain, the United Kingdom or, on a different level, of the possible future development of the European Union.

In fact, in the West, to speak today of nationalisms (majority or minority) is to speak of democracy. In other words, it is to speak of individual and collective rights; of institutions and of decision-making processes in different geographical areas – regions, states and supra-states; of the accommodation of different national symbols; of federalism and the division of powers; or of the legitimacy or not of incorporating processes of secession into the liberal-democratic rules of the game. With the present form of political liberalism, minority democratic nations such as Quebec, Scotland, Flanders or Catalonia, and their relationship with the plurinational democracies to which they belong – Canada, the United Kingdom, Belgium and Spain – cannot be adequately addressed using the premises and categories of nineteenth-century nationalisms. These nationalisms, in their state or stateless forms, tended to maintain an ambiguous relationship with liberal-democratic principles. This is in sharp contrast to the eminently liberal-democratic nature of majority and minority nationalisms of the political entities mentioned above. The concept of a uniform national democracy, based on the republican idea of a homogeneous and sovereign political unit is no longer adequate in plurinational contexts. This calls for differences in the descriptive and normative analyses of institutions and decision-making processes such as the rights of citizenship, parliamentarianism, federalism, foreign representation, and so on, depending on whether we are in uni-national or plurinational democracies.

The conclusion is that there has been no in-depth questioning of, on the one hand, what is meant by the implementation of the 'universal' values of democratic liberalism in states which are always particular and, on the other hand, the fact that there has been a marginalisation of the relationship between the processes of nation-building carried out or demanded by the different types of nationalism and liberal-democratic normativity. One thing that both aspects have in common is that it is assumed that there can be only one *demos* per democracy, in order perhaps to ignore the possibility of establishing a relationship between majority and minority national particularisms on an equal footing, or perhaps in order to justify secession processes that appear to lead to the establishment of as many democracies as there are national *demoi*. It is surprising, for example, how the main political theories of democratic liberalism, including most of the soundest and most refined ones from an intellectual perspective, such as those of Rawls and Habermas, display deficiencies when they have to deal with national pluralism. This is a question that is not so much badly resolved as completely unaddressed by the premises, concepts and normative questions of these theories. And this is despite the fact that, practically speaking, all liberal democracies have acted as nationalising agencies for specific cultural particularisms. So, it is the aim of this volume to identify the need to substitute this 'monist' conception of the democratic *demos* with one that is more 'pluralist' when dealing with plurinational democracies.

The link between the two main elements in this book – the revision of democratic liberalism and the practical political accommodation of plurinational polities – suggests that the challenges posed in the spheres of rights, symbols, institutions, competences or foreign affairs demands a revision of the interpretations of the liberal-democratic normativity itself. This revision should not be viewed as an *external confrontation* between 'democratic liberalism', on the one hand, and 'nationalism', on the other, but as a way of achieving an *internal accommodation,* in liberal-democratic terms, between distinct national collectives within the same polity. It also suggests that the practical constitutional implementation of this accommodation cannot be guaranteed only by the traditional regulation of civil, political and social rights of citizenship, which frequently results in a series of cultural biases that favour majority national groups.

The key question raised in the contributions to this volume is that of the normative and institutional *quality* of plurinational democracies in a globalised political, economic, technological and cultural context. In plurinational democracies, the quality of a democracy should go beyond the mere 'justice' of its institutions. It should include a sense of accommodation and solidarity between the different groups of which it is composed. We are clearly dealing with democracies with complex national identities, which pose questions of legitimacy that are different to those posed by uni-national democracies. In this context, what is at stake is a 'better' interpretation and a 'better' institutionalisation of the liberal-democratic values of liberty, equality, pluralism and dignity. This can be achieved by means of a political and constitutional recognition of democratic plurinationality and a form of self-government for the majority and the minority nations that is consistent with such a recognition. In other words, ways need to be found to improve those values that inhabit the spheres of rights, institutions and collective decision-making processes. We need a revision and a series of reforms that will minimise the risk that, to quote Shakespeare once more: 'Our thoughts are ours, their ends none of our own.'[2]

## Contributions to this volume

In Chapter 2 entitled 'The new debate over minority rights', Will Kymlicka analyses how discussion on minority rights in the sphere of Western political theory has evolved in the 1980s and 1990s. Four phases are identified. First, this discussion was established from a communitarian perspective. This is an approach which links up with classical debates of political thought on the priority of individual liberty. In this phase, the defence of minority rights meant accepting, to a large extent, the communitarian criticism of political liberalism. In contrast, the debate in the second phase is between liberals. Kymlicka points out that the debate in the earlier phase was deficient in its basic approach for two reasons: it misinterpreted the nature of cultural minorities and that of democratic liberalism itself. Although some empirical exceptions can be found, most minorities (immigrants, national stateless minorities, and others) do not wish to protect themselves from modernity, but to be recognised and participate in it on an equal footing. In the debate on minority rights, it is now proposed that cultural demands linked to identity require a revision of liberal principles, such as the notions of liberty and equality, that have arisen in basically homogeneous societies of the eighteenth and nineteenth centuries. This is where the author's well-known distinction between 'external protections' and 'internal restrictions' should be situated. The third phase approaches minority rights from a different perspective: as a response to the processes of state nation-building. The key point is a criticism of the alleged cultural neutrality of the principles that regulate the public sphere in democracies. Religion, Kymlicka tells us, may be treated neutrally by the liberal state; culture may not. As far as the latter is concerned, neutrality is false both conceptually and historically. In all democracies a series of nation-building processes are carried out. They are sometimes guided by a series of completely legitimate objectives (education, economic efficiency, welfare services) that involve implicit integration in a 'societal culture'. Here the debate is about the liberal or non-liberal nature of the process of nation-building. This question lays down two basic challenges: the need to construct an acceptable theory of nation-building, for both national majorities and minorities, from liberal premises, and the regulation of more just forms of political integration for immigrant minorities from the point of view of cultural identity. Finally, the author speculates about the beginning of a fourth phase based on the fact that critics of minority rights do not question their inherent 'justice', but the erosionary effects that they have on 'civic virtues' and practices linked with democratic 'citizenship'. Minority rights are not questioned because they are unjust, but because they destabilise, although, as the author points out, the critics fail to offer any empirical evidence that this is the case as far as democracies are concerned.

The current processes of nation-building of stateless nations is the issue addressed in Michael Keating's Chapter 3, 'Nations without states: minority nationalism in the global era'. The basic context of these processes is ruled by three transformations of the state: the construction of supra-state frameworks like the European Union and the North American Free Trade Agreement (NAFTA); the processes of deregulation and privatisation of the public sectors; and the emergence of sub-states as distinct political players. Despite the fact that the states retain a large part of their functional character, these three transformations signify an increasing interdependence between states, as well as an erosion of their legitimacy. In this context, the stateless nations must re-address their own processes of nation-building. Keating poses, first of all, the question of collective identity itself. The modernisation of the nationalisms is based on their ability to connect the past and the future, and through identities of a cultural rather than of an ethnical nature. Thus, linguistic policies, which are usually a central element in the process of nation-building are not established in order to achieve a single cultural code – as did, in most cases, the state nation-building movements of the nineteenth century – but in order to consolidate national identity while more plural situations, with bilingual and multiple-identity practices are established. Catalonia and Scotland display a higher level of coexistence, while Wales and the Basque Country are more divided societies. Quebec is somewhere in between these two. Second, constitutional options in order to exercise the right of self-determination (independence, sovereignty, confederation, plurinational federalism) show indecision that reflects uncertainty about the significance of independence and self-government in the world today. People's answers on the subject of independence depend on how the question is formulated. Third, the EU represents both an opportunity for the functional autonomy of European stateless nations, albeit through their respective states, and a new area for symbolic projection. Finally, the author points out the importance of territorial systems of production, and of processes of institution-building – by means of asymmetrical regulations – for the consolidation of stateless nations as more than just regions. Techniques of decentralisation are not enough for a political accommodation that recognises the multiple national identities that exist in some states, although the existence of frameworks like the EU offers greater chances to establish processes that combine elements of cooperation and competence.

Enric Fossas' Chapter 4, 'National plurality and equality', analyses one of the possible constitutional solutions mentioned in Chapter 3: plurinational federalism. The analysis hinges on the relationship between federalism and equality, a question which is always present in any political and academic debate about federalism, above all in plurinational states. After establishing a series of analytical distinctions, Fossas discusses political equality through its three classical senses in plurinational federations: equality among the founding groups of the federation; equality among federated units; and equality among the citizens of the federation. First, the evolution of plurinational societies and federalism reveals the limits of the latter as a framework for political accommodation in these societies. There are a number of processes linked to the development of modern states that have worked against equality among the founding groups of the federation. Among them are democratisation (civil equality), state interventionism, and the processes of nation-building. Second, the discussion about equality among the federated units often presents, in the case of plurinational federations, a clash between two incompatible conceptions of federalism. On the one hand, that which defends federal agreements as a way of expressing the different identities and the self-government of the national groups that coexist within the federation. In this case, one defends the suitability of establishing asymmetrical mechanisms when the society in question displays asymmetries in the national identities of its people. On the other hand, the conception that understands federalism as a technique for decentralising power, and whose aim is linked to the development of democracy or of the general efficiency of the political system. This clash is present in the debate on federalism in Belgium, Canada or Spain. Depending on the perspective adopted, the perception of the inequalities will be diametrically opposed. At the heart of the matter, there is a tension between understanding the political collectivity as a single, albeit culturally plural, reality, or understanding that what exists is a plurality of political collectivities (or of *demoi*). The contrast between these two visions reflects a process of competitive nation-building in which state nationalism has traditionally been very belligerent. Finally, Fossas deals with equality of citizenship, a concept that also has a tense relationship with the concept of federalism. The process of universalisation of rights has tended towards a standardisation between the citizens of the federations, albeit to a lesser degree than in non-federal states and not necessarily related to greater centralisation. From the perspective of national minorities, the criticism made is that behind universalism as a legitimising argument for democracies are the cultural values of the majorities. The argument of equality of citizenship, concludes Fossas, against the establishment of federal asymmetries is not acceptable. Following what Jeremy Weber pointed out a few years ago, asymmetry does not mean that the citizens of a federated state have more power than those of other states, it merely indicates where this power is exercised. In other words, asymmetry indicates that the territorial division of powers is established in a different way in some units than in others. Political and constitutional accommodation of plurinational realities demands a revision of the assumptions of the nation state and of federalism, as well as the idea of equality itself.

Wayne Norman's Chapter 5, 'Secession and (constitutional) democracy', analyses an aspect of this revision of democratic states demanded in Chapter 4: the legitimacy or not of secession in the case of plurinational societies, and the convenience of its inclusion in the constitutional mechanisms of the state. After pointing out that it does not seem very reasonable to postulate a direct inference between, on the one hand, self-determination and the rule of the majority and, on the other hand, secession, Norman criticises the arguments established by Cass Sunstein in order to oppose secession on the grounds that it is a mechanism that would produce distortions in the democratic process.

The key point is if secessionism would increase or decrease, a question on which it is difficult to generalise and which must therefore be analysed case by case. A 'just' regulation of secession should combine the will of the sub-unit of the state with a series of restrictive clauses, more than 50 per cent, which will discourage its 'tactical' use by nationalist organisations or leaders of minority groups. In fact, the author tells us, all federal constitutions allow for changes in the division of powers. Secession may be seen as the logical extreme of a number of characteristics that already exist in democratic federations. If it were not used, it would represent a legitimation of the state as an entity united not by force, but by consensus. Many states have not formed voluntarily. The inclusion of a constitutional procedure would not bring about a break with the rule of law. Norman establishes an analogy with divorce as a useful point of reference: it may become 'difficult', but it is unacceptable for the degree of difficulty to be unilaterally established by the stronger part only. An example of this is the ruling of the Canadian Supreme Court (October 1998) that established a secession clause, albeit incomplete and needing development by political actors, in the constitution. Liberal democracy is based not only on the principle of majority, but on four principles: federalism, democracy, constitutionalism (the rule of law), and respect for minorities. The court considers that a unilateral secession would violate these four principles, but at the same time rules in favour of the legitimacy of the process. Norman's conclusion is that the inclusion of secession in constitutional mechanisms is not only consistent with democratic federalism, but it may even be said to be one of its requirements.

Chapters 6 and 7 focus on the revision of the concept of 'democratic citizenship' within the plurinational and multicultural European Union. In 'National plurality within single statehood in the European Union', Carlos Closa addresses the issue of European citizenship from the perspective of globalisation and of a post-national universe in which notions of citizenship and nationality do not coincide, especially in the case of plurinational states. Whereas globalisation introduces a certain amount of relativism into the moral bases of the nation state, the European Union is obliged to overcome its initial functionalist approach – as the solution to a problem between European states – in order to take a step towards a more 'political' stage, increasingly supported by a discourse of democratic legitimacy. In this new context, which is still in its early stages, the notion of European citizenship based on the treaties of Maastricht and Amsterdam can be conceived only in terms that go beyond the legal and political framework of the nation states. Closa touches upon the methodological aspects relating to how to deal with European citizenship. He suggests a combination of inductive and deductive strategies of citizenship: the former permit the construction of a kind of map of the questions and issues that this concept involves, while the latter offer moral criteria that allow one to contrast the moral validity of the proposed solutions. Moreover, he defends the legitimacy of establishing guarantees for national minority rights within the institutional framework of the EU. These guarantees are currently not developed and it is certainly unclear that they may be regulated under the perspective of the so-called 'Europe of the Regions'. The institutional development of the EU in the near future may show a *statist* bias that can act against the legitimate rights of European national minorities (Scottish, Catalan, Flemish and others) to be recognised and institutionally protected. This also affects the case of immigrant peoples within the countries of the EU, which is the question addressed in Chapter 7.

In 'The limits of a multinational Europe: democracy and immigration in the European Union', Ricard Zapata addresses the question of immigration policies and the accommodation of immigrant peoples from a normative point of view. The main point is, again, to understand citizenship as a notion which is not linked to nationality. Using the approach of the 'spheres of justice' introduced by Michael Walzer, the author analyses the different roles that equality plays for immigrants in two different spheres: when they achieve citizenship and when they exercise this status. Zapata also offers three models for the accommodation of democratic citizenship for immigrant people: assimilationist, integrative and autonomous. These three models establish different versions of justice in the public sphere of multicultural democracies. The chapter goes on to analyse the case of the EU and of Spanish immigration laws, taking as a starting point the concept of 'Euro-foreigner' that does not take into account the original nationality of the immigrants, and which makes it possible to discriminate between the inequalities produced in the different state laws of the EU countries.

Finally, my own contribution, 'Democratic legitimacy and national pluralism', addresses a number of theoretical issues related to democratic legitimacy in plurinational polities. First of all, I discuss some linguistic components of present-day liberal-democratic legitimising theories. In the absence of a single all-encompassing theory of democratic legitimacy, every different approach stresses its own specific legitimising values and issues. These different approaches also imply a variety of interpretations of traditional concepts such as universality, equality, identity, as well as a variety of practical conclusions about what kinds of rights, institutions or decision-making processes should be considered 'just' in different democratic contexts. We are currently facing a form of normative pluralism in liberal democracies which is also linked to different kinds of uni-national or plurinational societies and which, I suggest, may be approached from the 'regulative ideas' of Kantian philosophy.

To sum up, the contributions included in this volume address most of the major questions of the conceptual and practical revision of plurinational liberal democracies at the beginning of the twenty-first century: political equality and citizenship; the cultural neutrality of the state; nationalism in the era of globalisation; the unavoidable collective dimension of individual rights; the adaptation of federalism to a much more complex world than that which existed when it was created, and, of course, the accommodation of different national collectivities in the public sphere of democratic polities and of recent suprastate political structures such as the European Union.

## Notes

1 *Romeo and Juliet*, Act 3, Scene 4.
2 *Hamlet*, Act 3, Scene 2.

Part I

# Minority rights and globalisation in multinational democracies

# 2 The new debate over minority rights

## Will Kymlicka

The 1990s saw a remarkable upsurge in interest among political philosophers in the rights of ethnocultural groups within Western democracies.[1] My aim in this chapter is to give a condensed overview of the philosophical debate so far, and to suggest some future directions that it might take.

Political philosophers are interested in the normative issues raised by such minority rights. What are the moral arguments for or against such rights? In particular, how do they relate to the underlying principles of liberal democracy, such as individual freedom, social equality and democracy? Are minority rights consistent with these principles? Do they promote these values? Or do they conflict with them?

The philosophical debate on these questions has changed dramatically, both in its scope and in its basic terminology. Prior to 1989, there were very few political philosophers or political theorists working in the area.[2] Indeed, for most of the twentieth century, issues of ethnicity have been seen as marginal by political philosophers. (Much the same can be said about many other academic disciplines, from sociology to geography to history.)

Today however, after decades of relative neglect, the question of minority rights has moved to the forefront of political theory. There are a number of reasons for this. Most obviously, the collapse of Communism in 1989 unleashed a wave of ethnic nationalisms in Eastern Europe which dramatically affected the democratisation process. Optimistic assumptions that liberal democracy would emerge smoothly from the ashes of Communism were derailed by issues of ethnicity and nationalism. But there were many factors within long-established Western democracies which also pointed to the salience of ethnicity: the nativist backlash against immigrants and refugees in many Western countries; the resurgence of indigenous peoples, resulting in the draft declaration of the rights of indigenous peoples at the

United Nations; and the ongoing, even growing, phenomenon of minority nationalism within some of the most flourishing Western democracies, from Quebec to Scotland, Flanders and Catalonia.

All of these factors, which came to a head at the beginning of the 1990s, made it clear that Western liberal democracies had not in fact resolved or overcome the tensions which ethnocultural diversity can raise. It is not surprising, therefore, that political theorists have increasingly turned their attention to this issue. For example, the 1990s witnessed the first philosophical books in English on the normative issues involved in secession, nationalism, immigration, multiculturalism, and indigenous rights.[3]

But the debate has not only grown in size. The very terms of the debate have also dramatically changed. I think we can distinguish four distinct stages in the debate.

### The first stage: minority rights as communitarianism

The first stage was the pre-1989 debate. Those few theorists who discussed the issue in the 1970s and 1980s assumed that the debate over minority rights was essentially equivalent to the debate between 'liberals' and 'communitarians' (or between 'individualists' and 'collectivists'). Confronted with an unexplored topic, it was natural, and perhaps inevitable, that political theorists would look for analogies with other, more familiar, topics, and the liberal–communitarian debate seemed the most relevant and applicable.

The liberal–communitarian debate is an old and venerable one within political philosophy, going back several centuries, albeit in different forms. So I will not try to rehearse the entire debate. But to oversimplify dramatically, the debate essentially revolves around the priority of individual freedom. Liberals insist that individuals should be free to decide on their own conception of the good life, and applaud the liberation of individuals from any ascribed or inherited status. Liberal individualists argue that the individual is morally prior to the community: the community matters only because it contributes to the well-being of the individuals who compose it. If those individuals no longer find it worthwhile to maintain existing cultural practices, then the community has no independent interest in preserving those practices, and no right to prevent individuals from modifying or rejecting them.

Communitarians dispute this conception of the 'autonomous individual'. They view individuals as 'embedded' in particular social roles and relationships, rather than as agents capable of forming and revising their own conception of the good life. Rather than viewing group practices as the product of individual choices, they tend to view individuals as the product of social practices. Moreover, they often deny that the interests of communities can be reduced to the interests of their individual members. Privileging individual autonomy is therefore seen as destructive of communities. A healthy community maintains a balance between individual choice and protection for the communal way of life, and seeks to limit the extent to which the former can erode the latter.

In this first stage of the debate, the assumption was that one's position on minority rights was dependent on, and derivative of, one's position on the liberal–communitarian debate. That is, if one is a liberal who cherishes individual autonomy, then one will oppose minority rights as an unnecessary and dangerous departure from the proper emphasis on the individual. Communitarians, by contrast, view minority rights as an appropriate way of protecting communities from the eroding effects of individual autonomy, and of affirming the value of community. Ethnocultural minorities in particular are worthy of such protection, partly because they are most at risk, but also because they still have a communal way of life to be protected. Unlike the majority, ethnocultural minorities have not yet succumbed to liberal individualism, and so have maintained a coherent collective way of life.

This debate over the priority and reducibility of community interests to individual interests dominated the early literature on minority rights. This interpretation of the debate was shared by both defenders and critics of minority rights[4]. Both sides agreed that in order to evaluate minority rights we needed to first resolve these ontological and metaphysical questions about the relative priority of individuals and groups. In short, defending minority rights involved endorsing the communitarian critique of liberalism, and viewing minority rights as defending cohesive and communally minded minority groups against the encroachment of liberal individualism.

## The second stage: minority rights within a liberal framework

It is increasingly recognised that this is an unhelpful way to conceptualise most minority rights claims in Western democracies. Equating minority rights with communitarianism seemed sensible at the time, but assumptions about the 'striking parallel between the communitarian attack of philosophical liberalism and the notion of collective rights' have been increasingly questioned (Galenkamp 1993: 20–5).

There are two problems with this approach: first, it misinterprets the nature of ethnocultural minorities; and second, it misinterprets the nature of liberalism.

In reality, most ethnocultural groups within Western democracies do not want to be protected from the forces of modernity unleashed in liberal societies (Frideres 1997; Harles 1993). On the contrary, they want to be full and equal participants in modern liberal societies. This is true of most immigrant groups, which seek inclusion and full participation in the mainstream of liberal-democratic societies, with access to its education, technology, literacy, mass communications, and so on. It is equally true of most non-immigrant national minorities, like the Québécois, Flemish or Catalans.[5] They may seek to secede from a liberal democracy, but if they do, it is not in order to create an illiberal communitarian society, but rather to create their own modern liberal-democratic society. The Québécois wish to create a 'distinct society', but it is a modern, liberal society – with an urbanised, secular, pluralistic, industrialised, bureaucratised, consumerist mass culture.[6]

Indeed, far from opposing liberal principles, public opinion polls show there are often no statistical differences between national minorities and majorities in their adherence to liberal principles.[7] And immigrants also quickly absorb the basic liberal-democratic consensus, even when they came from countries with little or no experience of liberal democracy.

To be sure, there are some important exceptions to this rule. For example, there are a few ethnoreligious sects which voluntarily distance themselves from the larger world – the Hutterites, Amish, Hasidic Jews. And perhaps some of the more isolated or traditionalist indigenous communities fit this description as 'communitarian' groups. The question of how liberal states should respond to such non-liberal groups is an important one, which I have discussed elsewhere (Kymlicka 1995a: ch. 8).

But the overwhelming majority of debates about minority rights are not debates between a liberal majority and communitarian minorities, but debates among liberals about the meaning of liberalism. They are debates between individuals and groups who endorse the basic liberal-democratic consensus, but who disagree about the interpretation of these principles in multiethnic societies – in particular, they disagree about the proper role of language, nationality, and ethnic identities within liberal-democratic societies and institutions.

This leads to the second problem with the pre-1989 debate – namely, the assumption that liberal principles are inherently opposed to minority rights claims. We now know that things are much more complicated, particularly under modern conditions of ethnocultural pluralism. We have inherited a set of assumptions about what liberal principles require, but these assumptions first emerged in eighteenth-century United States, or nineteenth-century England, where there was very little ethnocultural heterogeneity. Virtually all citizens shared the same language, ethnic descent, national identity, and Christian faith. It is increasingly clear that we cannot simply rely on the interpretation of liberalism developed in those earlier times and places. We need to judge for ourselves what liberalism requires under our own conditions of ethnocultural pluralism.

And defenders of minority rights insist that at least certain forms of public recognition and support for the language, practices and identities of minority groups are not only consistent with basic liberal-democratic principles, including the importance of individual autonomy, but may indeed be required by them.

This is the second stage of the debate – what is the possible scope for minority rights within liberal theory? Framing the debate this way does not resolve the issues. On the contrary, the place of minority rights within liberal theory remains very controversial. But it changes the terms of the debate. The question is no longer how to protect com-munitarian minorities from liberalism, but why minorities which share basic liberal principles nonetheless seek minority rights? If groups are indeed liberal, why do they want minority rights? Why are they not satisfied with the traditional common rights of citizenship?

This is the sort of question which Charles Taylor is trying to answer in his work on the importance of 'recognition' (Taylor 1992). He argues that people demand recognition for their differences, not instead of individual freedom, but rather as a support and precondition for freedom. Similarly, Joseph Raz, David Miller and Yael Tamir have all written about the importance of 'cultural membership' or 'national identity' to modern freedom-seeking citizens (Tamir 1993; Miller 1995; Margalit and Raz 1990; Raz 1994). In each case, the argument is made that there are compelling interests related to culture and identity, which are fully consistent with liberal principles of freedom and equality, and which justify granting 'special rights' to minorities.[8]

To be sure, we can easily imagine some forms of minority rights which would undermine, rather then support, individual autonomy. A crucial task facing liberal defenders of minority rights is to distinguish between the 'bad' minority rights which involve *restricting* individual rights, from the 'good' minority rights which can be seen as *supplementing* individual rights.

One way to draw this distinction is to consider two kinds of rights that a minority group might claim: the first involves the right of a group against its own members; the second involves the right of a group against the larger society. Both kinds of group rights can be seen as protecting the stability of national, ethnic or religious groups. However, they respond to different sources of instability. The first kind is intended to protect the group from the destabilising impact of *internal* dissent (e.g. the decision of individual members not to follow traditional practices or customs), whereas the second is intended to protect the group from the impact of *external* pressures (e.g. the economic or political decisions of the larger society). To distinguish these two kinds of group rights, we can call the first 'internal restrictions', and the second 'external protections'.

Given their commitment to protecting individual autonomy, liberals are very sceptical of claims to internal restrictions, but an increasing number of liberals are willing to give external protections a legitimate place within liberal-democratic theory. Various external protections – such as language rights, land rights, guarantees of group representation, exemptions from dress-codes and Sunday-closing legislation and so on – can be seen as supporting, rather than threatening, the autonomy of group members, by lessening their vulnerability to majoritarian political or economic power. And if it is true that minorities have themselves internalised liberal values, we would expect that they would primarily be seeking such external protections, rather than seeking the right to restrict the freedom of their own members to question or revise traditional cultural practices. And I believe that this is indeed what we see within most Western democracies: minorities overwhelmingly are seeking external protections, not internal restrictions (Kymlicka 1998: ch. 4).

In the second stage of the debate, therefore, the question of minority rights is reformulated as a question within liberal theory, and the aim is to show that some (but not all) minority rights claims actually enhance liberal values. In my opinion, this second stage reflects genuine progress. We now have a more accurate description of the claims being made by ethnocultural groups, and a more accurate understanding of the normative issues they raise. We have gotten beyond the sterile and misleading debate about individualism and collectivism.

However, I think this second stage also needs to be questioned and challenged. In particular, while it has a more accurate understanding of the nature of most ethnocultural groups, and the demands they place on the liberal state, it misinterprets the nature of the liberal state, and the demands it places on minorities.

## The third stage: minority rights as a response to nation-building

Let me explain. The assumption – generally shared by both defenders and critics of minority rights – is that the liberal state, in its normal operation, abides by a principle of ethnocultural neutrality. That is, the state is 'neutral' with respect to the ethnocultural identities of its citizens, and indifferent to the ability of ethnocultural groups to reproduce themselves over time. On this view, liberal states treat culture in the same way as religion – that is, as something which people should be free to pursue in their private life, but which is not the concern of the state (so long as they respect the rights of others). Just as liberalism precludes the establishment of an official religion, so too there cannot be official cultures which have preferred status over other possible cultural allegiances (Walzer 1992: 100–1).

Indeed, some theorists argue that this is precisely what distinguishes liberal 'civic nations' from illiberal 'ethnic nations' (Pfaff 1993: 162; Ignatieff 1993). Ethnic nations take the reproduction of a particular ethnonational culture and identity as one of their most important goals. Civic nations, by contrast, are 'neutral' with respect to the ethnocultural identities of their citizens, and define national membership purely in terms of adherence to certain principles of democracy and justice. For minorities to seek special rights, on this view, is a radical departure from the traditional operation of the liberal state. Therefore, the burden of proof lies on anyone who would wish to endorse such minority rights.

This is the burden of proof which Taylor tries to meet with his account of the importance of 'recognition'. Without minority rights, the group feels misrecognised, or simply invisible. And this is the burden of proof which Raz tries to meet with his account of the value of group 'membership' in securing self-respect. Both try to show that minority rights supplement, rather than diminish, individual freedom and equality, and help to meet needs which would otherwise go unmet in a state which clung rigidly to ethnocultural neutrality.

So in the second stage of the debate, the question is whether there are compelling reasons to depart from the norm or presumption of ethnocultural neutrality. As I noted, this way of interpreting the debate is largely shared by both defenders and critics.

I would argue, however, that this idea that liberal-democratic states (or 'civic nations') are ethnoculturally neutral is manifestly false, both historically and conceptually. The religion model is altogether misleading as an account of the relationship between the liberal-democratic state and ethnocultural groups.

Consider the actual policies of the United States, which is the allegedly prototypically 'neutral' state. First, it is a legal requirement for children to learn the English language in schools. Second, it is a legal requirement for immigrants (over the age of 50) to learn the English language to acquire American citizenship. Third, it is a de facto requirement for employment in or for government that the applicant speak English. Fourth, decisions about the boundaries of state governments, and the timing of their admission into the federation, were deliberately made to ensure that anglophones would be a majority within each of the fifty states of the American federation.

These decisions about the language of education and government employment, the requirements of citizenship, and the drawing of internal boundaries, are profoundly important. They are not isolated exceptions to some norm of ethnocultural neutrality. On the contrary, they are tightly interrelated, and together they have shaped the very structure of the American state, and the way the state structures society. (For example, since governments account for 40–50 per cent of gross national product (GNP) in most countries, the language of government employment and contracts is not negligible.)

These decisions were all made with the intention of promoting integration into what I call a 'societal culture'. By a societal culture, I mean a territorially concentrated culture, centred on a shared language which is used in a wide range of societal institutions, in both public and private life (schools, media, law, economy, government). I call it a *societal* culture to emphasise that it involves a common language and social institutions, rather than common religious beliefs, family customs or personal lifestyles. Societal cultures within a modern liberal democracy are inevitably pluralistic, containing Christians as well as Muslims, Jews and atheists; heterosexuals as well as gays; urban professionals as well as rural farmers; conservatives as well as socialists. Such diversity is the inevitable result of the rights and freedoms guaranteed to liberal citizens – including freedom of conscience, association, speech, political dissent and rights to privacy – particularly when combined with an ethnically diverse population.

The US government has deliberately promoted integration into such a societal culture – that is, it has encouraged citizens to view their life-chances as tied up with participation in common societal institutions that operate in the English language. Nor is the Unites States unique in this respect. Promoting integration into a societal culture is part of a 'nation-building' project which all liberal democracies have engaged in, although, as I discuss below, some countries have tried to sustain two or more societal cultures.

Obviously, the sense in which English-speaking Americans share a common 'culture' is a very thin one, since it does not preclude differences in religion, personal values, family relationships or lifestyle choices. Indeed, this use of the term 'culture' is in conflict with the way it is used in most academic disciplines, where culture is defined in a very thick, ethnographic sense, referring to the sharing of specific folk-customs, habits, and rituals. Citizens of a modern liberal state do not share a common culture in such a thick, ethnographic sense. But if we want to understand the nature of modern state-building, we need a very different, and thinner, conception of culture, which focuses on a common language and societal institutions.

While this sort of common culture is thin, it is far from trivial. On the contrary, as I discuss below, attempts to integrate people into such a common societal culture have often been met with serious resistance. Although integration in this sense leaves a great deal of room for both the public and private expression of individual and collective differences, some groups have nonetheless vehemently rejected the idea that they should view their life-chances as tied up with the societal institutions conducted in the majority's language.

So we need to replace the idea of an 'ethnoculturally neutral' state with a new model of a liberal democratic state – what I call the 'nation-building' model. While the idea of a culturally neutral state is a myth, this is not to say that governments can only promote one societal culture. It is possible for government policies to encourage the sustaining of two or more societal cultures within a single country – indeed, as I discuss below, this is precisely what characterises multi-nation states like Canada, Switzerland, Belgium or Spain.

However, historically, virtually all liberal democracies have, at one point or another, attempted to diffuse a single societal culture throughout all of its territory.[9] Nor should this be seen purely as a matter of cultural imperialism or ethnocentric prejudice. This sort of nation-building serves a number of important and legitimate goals. For example, a modern economy requires a mobile, educated and literate workforce. Standardised public education in a common language has often been seen as essential if all citizens are to have equal opportunity to work in this modern economy.

Also, participation in a common societal culture has often been seen as essential for generating the sort of solidarity required by a welfare state, since it promotes a sense of common identity and membership. Moreover, a common language has been seen as essential to democracy – how can 'the people' govern together if they cannot understand one another? In short, promoting integration into a common societal culture has been seen as essential to social equality and political cohesion in modern states.

Of course, this sort of nation-building can also be used to promote illiberal goals. As Margaret Canovan puts it, nationhood is like a 'battery' which makes states run – the existence of a common national identity motivates and mobilises citizens to act for common political goals – and these goals can be liberal or illiberal (Canovan 1996: 80). The 'battery' of nationalism can be used to promote liberal goals (such as social justice, democratisation, equality of opportunity, economic development) or illiberal goals (chauvinism, xenophobia, militarism, and unjust conquest). The fact that the battery of nationalism can be used for so many functions helps to explain why it has been so ubiquitous. Liberal reformers invoke nationhood to mobilise citizens behind projects of social justice (e.g. comprehensive health care or public schooling); illiberal authoritarians invoke nationhood to mobilise citizens behind attacks on alleged enemies of the nation, be they foreign countries or internal dissidents. This is why nation-building is just as common in authoritarian regimes in the West as in democracies. Consider Spain under Franco, or Greece or Latin America under the military dictators. Authoritarian regimes also need a 'battery' to help achieve public objectives in complex modern societies. What distinguishes liberal from illiberal states is not the presence or absence of nation-building, but rather the ends to which nation-building is put.

So states have engaged in this process of 'nation-building' – that is, a process of promoting a common language, and a sense of common membership in, and equal access to, the social institutions based on that language.[10] Decisions regarding official languages, core curriculum in education, and the requirements for acquiring citizenship, all were made with the express intention of diffusing a particular culture throughout society, and of promoting a particular national identity based on participation in that societal culture.

If I am right that this nation-building model provides a more accurate account of the nature of modern liberal democratic states, how does this affect the issue of minority rights? I believe it gives us a very different perspective on the debate. The question is no longer how to justify departure from a norm of neutrality, but rather do majority efforts at nation-building create injustices for minorities? And do minority rights help protect against these injustices?

This would be the third stage in the debate, which I am trying to promote. I cannot explore all of its implications, but let me give two examples of how this new model of the liberal state may affect the debate over minority rights.

## Two examples

How does nation-building affect minorities? As Charles Taylor notes, the process of nation-building inescapably privileges members of the majority culture:

> If a modern society has an 'official' language, in the fullest sense of the term, that is, a state-sponsored, -inculcated, and -defined language and culture, in which both economy and state function, then it is obviously an immense advantage to people if this language and culture are theirs. Speakers of other languages are at a distinct disadvantage.
>
> (Taylor 1997: 34)

This means that minority cultures face a choice. If all public institutions are being run in another language, minorities face the danger of being marginalised from the major economic, academic, and political institutions of the society. Faced with this dilemma, minorities have (to over-simplify) three basic options:

• they can accept integration into the majority culture, although perhaps attempt to renegotiate the terms of integration;
• seek the sorts of rights and powers of self-government needed to maintain their own societal culture – that is to create their own economic, political and educational institutions in their own language. That is, engage in their own form of competing nation-building;
• accept permanent marginalisation.

We can find some ethnocultural groups which fit each of these categories (and other groups which are caught between them). For example, some immigrant groups choose permanent marginalisation. This would seem to be true, for example, of the Hutterites in Canada, or the Amish in the United States. But the option of accepting marginalisation is likely to be attractive only to religious sects whose theology requires them to avoid all contact with the modern world. The Hutterites and Amish are unconcerned about their marginalisation from universities or legislatures, since they view such 'worldly' institutions as corrupt.

Virtually all other ethnocultural minorities, however, seek to participate in the modern world, and to do so, they must either integrate or
seek the self-government needed to create and sustain their own
modern institutions. Faced with this choice, ethnocultural groups
have responded in different ways.

## National minorities

National minorities have typically responded to majority nation-
building by engaging in their own competing nation-building. Indeed,
they often use the same tools that the majority uses to promote this
nation-building – for example, control over the language and curriculum of schooling, the language of government employment, the requirements of immigration and naturalisation, and the drawing of internal
boundaries.

One way to acquire and exercise these nation-building powers is
through federalisation of the state, in order to create subunits in
which the national minority forms a local majority. Control over a
federal subunit enables a national minority to both resist state
nation-building, and to engage in their own competing substate
nation-building. And indeed there is a striking tendency for democratic
multination states to adopt federalism.[11]

We can see this clearly in the case of Québécois nationalism, which
has largely been concerned precisely with gaining and exercising these
nation-building powers at the provincial level. But it is also increasingly
true of the Aboriginal peoples in Canada, who have adopted the
language of 'nationhood', and who have established a quasi-federal
or 'federacy' status for their tribal governments. And the idea that
relations with Aboriginals should be conducted on a 'nation-to-nation'
basis has been affirmed by Canada's recent Royal Commission on
Aboriginal Peoples (RCAP). As the Commission notes, this first step
towards making such a model work is for Aboriginal peoples to
engage in a major campaign of 'nation-building', which requires the
exercise of much greater powers of self-government, and the building
of many new societal institutions.[12]

Intuitively, the adoption of such minority nation-building projects
seems fair. If the majority can engage in legitimate nation-building,
why not national minorities, particularly those which have been
involuntarily incorporated into a larger state? To be sure, liberal
principles set limits on *how* national groups go about nation-building.
Liberal principles will preclude any attempts at ethnic cleansing, or
stripping people of their citizenship, or the violation of human rights.

These principles will also insist that any national group engaged in a project of nation-building must respect the right of other nations within its jurisdiction to protect and build their own national institutions. For example, the Québécois are entitled to assert national rights *vis-à-vis* the rest of Canada, but only if they respect the rights of Aboriginals within Quebec to assert national rights *vis-à-vis* the rest of Quebec.

These limits are important, but they still leave significant room, I believe, for legitimate forms of minority nationalism. Moreover, these limits are likely to be similar for both majority and minority nations. All else being equal, national minorities should have the same tools of nation-building available to them as the majority nation, subject to the same liberal limitations.

What we need, in other words, is a consistent theory of permissible forms of nation-building within liberal democracies. I do not think that political theorists have yet developed such a theory. One of the many unfortunate side-effects of the dominance of the 'ethnocultural neutrality' model of the liberal state is that liberal theorists have never explicitly confronted this question.

I do not have a fully developed theory about the permissible forms of nation-building, and I suspect that this will prove to be a very controversial question.[13] My aim here is not to promote any particular theory of permissible nation-building, but simply to insist that this is the relevant question we need to address. That is, the question is not 'have national minorities given us a compelling reason to abandon the norm of ethnocultural neutrality?', but rather 'why should national minorities not have the same powers of nation-building as the majority?' This is the context within which minority nationalism must be evaluated – as a response to majority nation-building, using the same tools of nation-building. And the burden of proof surely rests on those who would deny national minorities the same powers of nation-building as those which the national majority takes for granted.

### Immigrants

Historically, nation-building has been neither desirable nor feasible for immigrant groups. Instead, they have traditionally accepted the expectation that they will integrate into the larger societal culture. Indeed, few immigrant groups have objected to the requirement that they must learn an official language as a condition of citizenship, or that their children must learn the official language in school. They have accepted the assumption that their life-chances, and even more the life-chances of their children, will be bound up with participation in mainstream institutions operating in the majority language.

However, immigrants can demand fairer terms of integration. For example, if Canada is going to pressure immigrants to integrate into common institutions operating in either English or French, then we need to ensure that the terms of integration are fair. To my mind, this demand has two basic elements: first, we need to recognise that integration does not occur overnight, but is a difficult and long-term process which operates intergenerationally. This means that special accommodations are often required for immigrants on a transitional basis. For example, certain services should be available in the immigrants' mother tongue, and support should be provided for those organisations and groups within immigrant communities which assist in the settlement and integration process. Second, we need to ensure that the common institutions into which immigrants are pressured to integrate provide the same degree of respect, recognition and accommodation of the identities and practices of ethnocultural minorities as they traditionally have been of WASP (White Anglo-Saxon Protestant) and French-Canadian identities. Otherwise, the promotion of English and French as official languages is tantamount to privileging the interests and lifestyles of the descendants of the English or French settlers.

This requires a systematic exploration of our social institutions to see whether their rules, structures and symbols disadvantage immigrants. For example, we need to examine dress codes, public holidays, or even height and weight restrictions to see whether they are biased against certain immigrant groups. We also need to examine the portrayal of minorities in school curricula or the media to see if they are stereotypical, or fail to recognise the contributions of ethnocultural groups to Canadian history or world culture. And so on.

These measures are needed to ensure that Canada is offering immigrants fair terms of integration. The idea of 'multiculturalism within a bilingual framework' is, I think, precisely an attempt to define such fair terms of integration. And in my view, the vast majority of what is done under the heading of multiculturalism policy, not only at the federal level, but also at provincial and municipal levels, and indeed within school boards and private companies, can be defended as promoting fair terms of integration (Kymlicka 1998: ch. 3).

Others may disagree with the fairness of some of these policies. The requirements of fairness are not always obvious, particularly in the context of people who have chosen to enter a country, and political theorists have done little to date to illuminate the issue. Here again, the dominance of the 'ethnocultural neutrality' model of the liberal state has blinded liberal theorists to the importance of the question. My aim here is not to promote a particular theory of fair terms of integration, but rather to insist that this is the relevant question we need to address. The question is not whether immigrants have given us a compelling reason to diverge from the norm of ethnocultural neutrality, but rather how can we ensure that state policies aimed at pressuring immigrants to integrate are fair?

The focus of this third stage of the debate, therefore, is to show how particular minority rights claims are related to, and a response to, state nation-building policies. And the logical outcome of this stage of the debate will be to develop theories of permissible nation-building and fair terms of integration. I expect that filling in these lacunae will form the main agenda for minority rights theorists over the next decade.

## A fourth stage?

As we can see, there have been several significant changes over a relatively short period of time in the minority rights debate. However, there has been an important assumption which is common to all three stages of the debate: namely, that the goal is to assess the *justice* of claims by minorities for the accommodation of their cultural differences. This focus on justice reflects the fact that opposition to minority rights claims has traditionally been stated in the language of justice. Critics of minority rights had long argued that justice required state institutions to be 'colour-blind'. To ascribe rights or benefits on the basis of membership in ascriptive groups was seen as inherently morally arbitrary and discriminatory, necessarily creating first and second-class citizens.

The first task confronting any defender of minority rights, therefore, was to try to overcome this presumption, and to show that deviations from difference-blind rules which are adopted in order to accommodate ethnocultural differences are not inherently unjust. As we have seen, this has been done in two main ways: by identifying the many ways that mainstream institutions are not neutral, but rather are implicitly or explicitly tilted towards the needs, interests and identities of the majority group; and by emphasising the importance of certain interests which have typically been ignored by liberal theories of justice – for example, interests in recognition, identity, language and cultural membership. If these interests are ignored or trivialised by the state, then people will feel harmed – and indeed will be harmed – even if their civil, political and welfare rights are respected, and the result can be serious damage to people's self-respect and sense of agency. If we accept either or both of these points, then we can see minority rights not as unfair privileges or invidious forms of discrimination, but rather as compensation for unfair disadvantages, and so as consistent with, and even required by, justice.

In my view, this debate over justice, which has been the main focus of the first three stages, is drawing to a close. Of course, as I noted earlier, much work remains to be done in assessing the justice of particular forms of immigrant multiculturalism or minority nationalism. But in terms of the more general question of whether minority rights are *inherently* unjust, the debate is essentially over, and the defenders of minority rights have won the day. I do not mean that the defenders of minority rights have been successful in getting their claims accepted and implemented, although there is a clear trend throughout the Western democracies towards greater recognition of minority rights. Rather I mean that defenders of minority rights have successfully redefined the terms of public debate in two profound ways. First, few thoughtful people continue to think that justice can simply be *defined* in terms of difference-blind rules or institutions. Instead, it is now widely recognised that difference-blind rules and institutions can cause disadvantages for particular groups. Whether justice requires common rules for all, or differential rules for diverse groups, is something to be assessed case-by-case in particular contexts, not assumed in advance. Second, as a result, the burden of proof has shifted. The burden of proof no longer falls solely on defenders of minority rights to show that their proposed reforms would not create injustices; the burden of proof equally falls on defenders of difference-blind institutions to show that the status quo does not create injustices for minority groups.

Defenders of minority rights have, in other words, punctured the complacency with which liberals used to dismiss claims for minority rights, and have successfully levelled the playing field when debating the merits of these claims. So the original justice-based grounds for blanket opposition to minority rights have faded. This has not meant that opposition to minority rights has disappeared, or even significantly diminished. But it now takes a new form: critics have shifted the focus away from justice towards issues of citizenship, focusing not on the justice or injustice of particular policies, but rather on the way that the general trend towards minority rights threatens to erode the sorts of civic virtues and citizenship practices which sustain a healthy democracy.

This focus on civic virtue and political stability represents, I think, the opening of a new front in the 'multiculturalism wars', and can be seen as a fourth stage in the debate. Many critics claim that minority rights are misguided, not because they are unjust in themselves, but rather because they are corrosive of long-term political unity and social stability. They may promote justice in principle, but in practice they are dangerous.[14]

Why are minority rights policies seen as destabilising? Different authors offer different answers, but the underlying worry is that minority rights involve the 'politicisation of ethnicity', and that any measures which heighten the salience of ethnicity in public life are divisive. Over time they create a spiral of competition, mistrust and antagonism between ethnic groups. Policies which increase the salience of ethnic identities are said to act 'like a corrosive on metal, eating away at the ties of connectedness that bind us together as a nation' (Ward 1991: 598). On this view, liberal democracies must prevent ethnic identities from becoming politicised by rejecting any minority rights approaches which involve the explicit public recognition of ethnic groups.

The extreme version of this critique treats minority rights as the first step on the road to Yugoslavia-style civil war. The idea that minority rights within Western democracies could lead to civil war is almost too silly to be worth discussing. But there is a more modest version of this criticism which is worth considering, and which is often phrased in the language of *citizenship*.

Minority rights, on this view, may not lead to civil war, but they will erode the ability of citizens to fulfil their responsibilities as democratic citizens: they will erode their ability to communicate, trust, and feel solidarity across group differences. And so even if a particular minority right claim is not itself unjust, examined in isolation, the trend towards the increased salience of ethnicity will erode the norms and practices of responsible citizenship, and so reduce the overall functioning of the state.

This is a serious concern. It is clear that the health and stability of a modern democracy depends, not only on the justice of its basic institutions, but also on the qualities and attitudes of its citizens, such as their sense of identity, and how they view potentially competing forms of national, regional, ethnic or religious identities; their ability to tolerate and work together with others who are different from themselves; their desire to participate in the political process in order to promote the public good and hold political authorities accountable; their willingness to show self-restraint and exercise personal responsibility in their political demands and in personal choices; and their sense of justice and commitment to a fair distribution of resources. Without citizens who possess these qualities, 'the ability of liberal societies to function successfully progressively diminishes' (Galston 1991: 220).[15]

There is growing fear that the public-spiritedness of citizens of liberal democracies may be in serious decline. And if group-based claims would further erode the sense of shared civic purpose and solidarity, then that would be a powerful reason not to adopt minority rights policies.

While I agree that this is an important issue that needs to be investigated, I also suspect that many of these claims about the erosion of citizenship are not entirely in good faith. It is interesting to note that many of the same people who used to argue vehemently that minority rights were unjust in principle, now argue with equal vehemence that while these rights may be just in principle, they are dangerous in practice.

Still, we cannot ignore this worry that minority rights will erode the norms and practices of responsible democratic citizenship. But is it true? There has been much armchair speculation on this question, but remarkably little evidence. We need reliable evidence about the deleterious impact of minority rights on citizenship because one could quite plausibly argue the reverse: namely, that it is the *absence* of minority rights which erodes the bonds of civic solidarity. After all, if we accept the two central claims made by defenders of minority rights – that is that mainstream institutions are biased in favour of the majority, and that the effect of this bias is to harm important interests related to personal agency and identity – then we might expect minorities to feel excluded from 'difference-blind' mainstream institutions, and to feel alienated from, and distrustful of, the political process. We could predict, then, that recognising minority rights would actually strengthen solidarity and promote political stability, by removing the barriers and exclusions which prevent minorities from wholeheartedly embracing political institutions. This hypothesis is surely at least as plausible as the contrary hypothesis that minority rights erode citizenship.

We do not yet have the sort of systematic evidence needed to decisively confirm or refute these competing hypotheses. However, there is fragmentary evidence suggesting that minority rights often enhance, rather than erode, responsible citizenship. For example, the evidence from Canada and Australia – the two countries which first adopted official multiculturalism policies for immigrants – strongly disputes the claim that immigrant multiculturalism promotes ethnic separatism, political apathy or instability, or the mutual hostility of ethnic groups. On the contrary, these two countries do a better job integrating immigrants into common civic and political institutions than any other country in the world. Moreover, both have witnessed dramatic reductions in the level of prejudice, and dramatic increases in the levels of interethnic friendships and intermarriage. There is no evidence that the pursuit of fairer terms of integration for immigrants has eroded citizenship (Kymlicka 1998: ch. 2).

The situation regarding the self-government claims of national minorities is more complicated, since these claims involve building separate institutions, and reinforcing a distinct national identity, and hence create the phenomenon of competing nationalisms within a single state. Learning how to manage this phenomenon is a profoundly difficult task for any multination state. However, even here there is significant evidence that recognising self-government for national minorities assists, rather than threatens, political stability. Indeed, surveys of ethnic conflict around the world repeatedly confirm that 'early, generous devolution is far more likely to avert than to abet ethnic separatism' (Horowitz 1991: 224). It is the refusal to grant autonomy to national minorities, or even worse, the decision to retract an already-existing autonomy (as in Kosovo), which leads to instability, not the recognising of their minority rights (Gurr 1993; Lapidoth 1996).[16]

Much more work needs to be done concerning the impact of minority rights on responsible citizenship and political stability. This relationship will undoubtedly vary from case to case, and so requires fine-grained empirical investigation. Even if this sort of work is more likely to be done by sociologists than philosophers, I suspect that theorists of minority rights will increasingly pay careful attention to the findings of social scientists on this topic. But as with concerns about justice, it is clear that concerns about citizenship cannot provide any grounds for rejecting minority rights *in general*: there is no reason to assume in advance that there is any inherent contradiction between minority rights and democratic citizenship.

## Conclusion

I have tried to outline four stages in the ongoing philosophical debate about minority rights. The first stage viewed minority rights as a tool communitarian groups can use to defend themselves against the encroachment of liberalism. This has gradually given way to a more recent debate regarding the role of culture and identity within liberalism itself. In this second stage of the debate, the question is whether people's interests in their culture and identity are sufficient to justify departing from the norm of ethnocultural neutrality, by supplementing common individual rights with minority rights.

This second stage represents progress, I think, in that it asks the right question, but it starts from the wrong baseline, since liberal democracies do not in fact abide by any norm of ethnocultural neutrality. And so the next stage of the debate, I propose, is to view minority rights, not as a deviation from ethnocultural neutrality, but as a response to majority nation-building. And I have suggested that this will affect the way we think of the demands of both national minorities and immigrant groups. In particular, it raises two profoundly important questions: what are permissible forms of nation-building; and what are fair terms of integration for immigrants?

Much work remains to be done in assessing the justice of particular minority rights claim. Today, however, we can see the emergence of a fourth stage, in which issues of justice are supplemented with issues of civic identity and political stability. These new considerations will make the debate even more complex, and resistant to easy formulas.

Looking back over the development of this debate, I am inclined to think that genuine progress has been made, although much remains to be done. It is progress, not in the sense of getting clearer answers, but rather in the sense of getting clearer on the *questions*. The emerging debates about the role of language, culture, ethnicity and nationality with liberal democracies are, I think, grappling in a fruitful way with the real issues facing ethnoculturally plural societies today. But getting clearer on the questions is no guarantee of getting clearer on the answers. Indeed, questions from all four of the stages remain unresolved: there is no consensus on the status of non-liberal groups within liberal-democracies (stage 1); or the link between culture and freedom (stage 2); the relationship between minority rights and nation-building (stage 3); or the link between minority rights and stability (stage 4). These debates will be with us for a long time to come.

## Notes

1 I use the term 'rights of ethnocultural minorities' (or, for brevity's sake, 'minority rights') in a loose way, to refer to a wide range of public policies, legal rights and exemptions, and constitutional provisions from multiculturalism policies to multination federalism, language rights and constitutional protections of Aboriginal treaties. This is a heterogeneous category, but they have two important features in common: they go beyond the familiar set of common civil and political rights of individual citizenship which are protected in all liberal democracies; and they are adopted with the intention of recognising and accommodating the distinctive identities and needs of ethnocultural groups. For a helpful typology, see Levy 1997.

2 The most important of whom was Vernon Van Dyke, who published a handful of essays on this topic in the 1970s and early 1980s (Van Dyke 1977, 1982, 1985). There were also a few legal theorists who discussed the role of minority rights in international law, and their connection to human rights principles of non-discrimination.

3 Baubock 1994; Buchanan 1991; Canovan 1996; Carens 2000; Gilbert 1998; Kymlicka 1995a; Kymlicka 2000; Levy 2000; Miller 1995; Parekh 2000; Phillips 1995; Spinner 1994; Tamir 1993; Taylor 1992; Tully 1995; Walzer 1997; Young 1990. I am not aware of full-length books written by philosophers in English on any of these topics predating 1990. For collections of recent philosophical articles on these issues, see Kymlicka 1995b; Baker 1994; McDonald 1991a; van Willigenburg and van der Burg 1995; Raikka 1996; McKim and McMahan 1997; Shapiro and Kymlicka 1997; Lehning 1998; Couture *et al.* 1998; Moore 1998; Beiner 1998; Schwartz 1995; Kymlicka and Norman 2000.

4 For representatives of the 'individualist' camp, see Jan Narveson (1991); Michael Hartney (1995). For the 'communitarian' camp, see the work of Vernon Van Dyke (1977, 1982); Ronald Garet (1983); Michael McDonald (1991a, 1991b); Darlene Johnston (1989); Adeno Addis (1991); Myron Gochnauer (1991); Dimitrios Karmis (1993); Frances Svennson (1979), all of whom defend minority rights from a communitarian perspective.

5 By national minorities, I mean groups which formed complete and functioning societies on their historic homeland prior to being incorporated into a larger state. The incorporation of such national minorities has typically been involuntary, due to colonisation, conquest, or the ceding of territory from one imperial power to another, but may also arise voluntarily, as a result of federation.

6 On the shift towards a modern and liberal nature of minority nationalisms in the West, see Chapter 3 by Michael Keating cf. Dion (1991).

7 See Kymlicka 2001: chs 11–15.

8 On this movement to reinterpret the role of culture in liberal theory, see the discussion of 'liberalism 1' and 'liberalism 2' in Chapter 8 by Ferran Requejo.

9 To my knowledge, Switzerland is perhaps the only exception: it never made any serious attempt to pressure its French and Italian minorities to integrate into the German majority. All of the other contemporary

Western multination states have at one time or another made a concerted
effort to assimilate their minorities, and only reluctantly gave up this ideal.

10 For the ubiquity of this process, see Gellner 1983; Anderson 1983.

11 Indeed Alfred Stepan claims that 'every single longstanding democracy in a
territorially based multilingual and multinational polity is a federal state'
(Stepan 1999: 19). On the relationship between federalism and nation-
building, see Chapter 4 by Enric Fossas.

12 On the adoption of the language of nationhood by Aboriginal peoples, see
Jenson 1993; Alfred 1995; RCAP 1996.

13 I have taken some tentative first steps towards developing a theory which
would enable us to distinguish liberal from illiberal forms of nation-
building in Kymlicka and Opalski 2001.

14 I should emphasise that justice and stability are not mutually exclusive
concerns. On the contrary, any plausible conception of justice must take
into account considerations of long-term stability. The institutions recommended by the theory must be capable of generating and sustaining their
own loyalty and support. Just institutions should be self-sustaining in this
way.

15 It is only recently that political philosophers have started to take this issue
of civic virtue and responsibility seriously. For a survey of this recent work
on citizenship within contemporary political philosophy, see Kymlicka
and Norman 2000.

16 For a discussion of political legitimacy in multination states, see Ferran
Requejo's Chapter 8.

# References

Addis, Adeno (1991) 'Individualism, Communitarianism and the Rights of
Ethnic Minorities', *Notre Dame Law Review* 67/3, pp. 615–76.

Alfred, Gerald (1995) *Heeding the Voices of our Ancestors: Kahnawake
Mohawk Politics and the Rise of Native Nationalism*, Toronto: Oxford
University Press.

Anderson, Benedict (1983) *Imagined Communities: Reflections on the Origin
and Spread of Nationalism*, London: New Left Books.

Baker, Judith (ed.) (1994) *Group Rights*, Toronto: University of Toronto
Press.

Baubock, Rainer (1994) *Transnational Citizenship: Membership and Rights in
Transnational Migration*, Aldershot: Edward Elgar.

Beiner, Ronald (ed.) (1998) *Theorizing Nationalism*, Albany, NY: SUNY
Press.

Buchanan, Allen (1991) *Secession: The Legitimacy of Political Divorce*,
Boulder, Col.: Westview Press.

Canovan, Margaret (1996) *Nationhood and Political Theory*, Cheltenham:
Edward Elgar.

Carens, Joseph H. (2000) *Culture, Citizenship and Community: A Con-
textural Exploration of Justice as Evenhandedness*, Oxford: Oxford University Press.

Couture, Jocelyne, Kai Nielsen and Michel Seymour (eds) (1998) *Rethinking Nationalism*, Calgary: University of Calgary Press.

Dion, Stéphane (1991) 'Le Nationalisme dans la Convergence Culturelle', in R. Hudon and R. Pelletier (eds) *L'Engagement intellectuel: Melanges en l'honneur de Léon Dion*, Sainte-Foy, Quebec: Les Presses de l'Université Laval.

Frideres, James (1997) 'Edging into the Mainstream: Immigrant Adults and their Children', in S. Isajiw (ed.) *Comparative Perspectives on Interethnic Relations and Social Incorporation in Europe and North America*, Toronto: Canadian Scholar's Press.

Galenkamp, Marlies (1993) *Individualism and Collectivism: The Concept of Collective Rights*, Rotterdam: Rotterdamse Filosofische Studies.

Galston, William (1991) *Liberal Purposes: Goods, Virtues, and Duties in the Liberal State*, Cambridge: Cambridge University Press.

Garet, Ronald (1983) 'Communality and Existence: The Rights of Groups', *Southern California Law Review* 56/5, pp. 1001–75.

Gellner, Ernest (1983) *Nations and Nationalism*, Oxford: Blackwell.

Gilbert, Paul (1998) *Philosophy of Nationalism*, Boulder, Col.: Westview Press.

Gochnauer, Myron (1991) 'Philosophical Musings on Persons, Groups, and Rights', *University of New Brunswick Law Journal* 40/1, pp. 1–20.

Gurr, Ted (1993) *Minorities at Risk: A Global View of Ethnopolitical Conflict*, Washington, DC: Institute of Peace Press.

Harles, John (1993) *Politics in the Lifeboat: Immigrants and the American Democratic Order*, Boulder, Col.: Westview Press.

Hartney, Michael (1995) 'Some Confusions Concerning Collective Rights', in Will Kymlicka (ed.) *The Rights of Minority Cultures*, Oxford: Oxford University Press.

Horowitz, Donald (1991) *A Democratic South Africa: Constitutional Engineering in a Divided Society*, Berkeley, Calif.: University of California Press.

Ignatieff, Michael (1993) *Blood and Belonging: Journeys into the New Nationalism*, New York: Farrar, Straus & Giroux.

Jenson, Jane (1993) 'Naming Nations: Making Nationalist Claims in Canadian Public Discourse', *Canadian Review of Sociology and Anthropology* 30/3, pp. 337–57.

Johnston, Darlene (1989) 'Native Rights as Collective Rights: A Question of Group Self-Preservation', *Canadian Journal of Law and Jurisprudence* 2/1, pp. 19–34.

Karmis, Dimitrios (1993) 'Cultures autochtones et libéralisme au Canada: les vertus mediatrices du communautarisme libéral de Charles Taylor', *Canadian Journal of Political Science* 26/1, pp. 69–96.

Kymlicka, Will (1989) *Liberalism, Community, and Culture*, Oxford: Oxford University Press.

Kymlicka, Will (1995a) *Multicultural Citizenship: A Liberal Theory of Minority Rights*, Oxford: Oxford University Press.

Kymlicka, Will (1995b) *The Rights of Minority Cultures*, Oxford: Oxford University Press.

Kymlicka, Will (1998) *Finding our Way: Rethinking Ethnocultural Relations in Canada*, Toronto: Oxford University Press.

Kymlicka, Will (2001) *Politics in the Vernacular: Nationalism, Multiculturalism, Citizenship*, Oxford: Oxford University Press.

Kymlicka, Will and Wayne Norman (eds) (2000) *Citizenship in Diverse Societies*, Oxford: Oxford University Press.

Kymlicka, Will and Magda Opalski (eds) (2001) *Can Liberal Pluralism be Exported?* Oxford: Oxford University Press.

Lapidoth, Ruth (1996) *Autonomy: Flexible Solutions to Ethnic Conflict*, Washington, DC: Institute for Peace Press.

Lehning, Percy (ed.) (1998) *Theories of Secession*, London: Routledge.

Levy, Jacob (1997) 'Classifying Cultural Rights', in Ian Shapiro and Will Kymlicka (eds), *Ethnicity and Group Rights*, New York: New York University Press.

Levy, Jacob (2000) *The Multiculturalism of Fear*, Oxford: Oxford University Press.

McDonald, Michael (1991a) 'Questions about Collective Rights', in D. Schneiderman (ed.) *Language and the State: The Law and Politics of Identity*, Montreal: Les Editions Yvon Blais.

McDonald, Michael (1991b) 'Should Communities have Rights? Reflections on Liberal Individualism', *Canadian Journal of Law and Jurisprudence* 4/2, pp. 217–37.

McKim, Robert and Jeff McMahan (eds) (1997) *The Morality of Nationalism*, New York: Oxford University Press.

Margalit, Avishai and Joseph Raz (1990) 'National Self-Determination', *Journal of Philosophy* 87/9, pp. 439–61.

Miller, David (1995) *On Nationality*, Oxford: Oxford University Press.

Moore, Margaret (ed.) (1998) *National Self-Determination and Secession*, Oxford: Oxford University Press.

Narveson, Jan (1991) 'Collective Rights?', *Canadian Journal of Law and Jurisprudence* 4/2, pp. 329–45.

Parekh, Bhikhu (2000) *Rethinking Multiculturalism: Cultural Diversity and Political Theory*, Cambridge, Mass.: Harvard University Press.

Pfaff, William (1993) *The Wrath of Nations: Civilization and the Furies of Nationalism*, New York: Simon & Schuster.

Phillips, Anne (1995) *The Politics of Presence: Issues in Democracy and Group Representation*, Oxford: Oxford University Press.

Raikka, Juha (ed.) (1996) *Do We Need Minority Rights: Conceptual Issues*, The Hague: Kluwer.

Raz, Joseph (1994) 'Multiculturalism: A Liberal Perspective', *Dissent*, Winter, pp. 67–79.

Royal Commission on Aboriginal Peoples (RCAP) (1996) *Report of the Royal Commission on Aboriginal Peoples. Volume 2: Restructuring the Relationship*, Ottawa: RCAP.

Schwartz, Warren (ed.) (1995) *Justice in Immigration*, Cambridge: Cambridge University Press.

Shapiro, Ian and Will Kymlicka (eds) (1997) *Ethnicity and Group Rights: NOMOS 39*, New York: New York University Press.

Spinner, Jeff (1994) *The Boundaries of Citizenship: Race, Ethnicity and Nationality in the Liberal State*, Baltimore, Md: Johns Hopkins University Press.

Stepan, Alfred (1999) 'Federalism and Democracy: Beyond the US Model', *Journal of Democracy*, 10/4, pp. 19–34.

Svensson, Frances (1979) 'Liberal Democracy and Group Rights: The Legacy of Individualism and its Impact on American Indian Tribes', *Political Studies* 27/3, pp. 421–39.

Tamir, Yael (1993) *Liberal Nationalism*, Princeton, NJ: Princeton University Press.

Taylor, Charles (1992) 'The Politics of Recognition', in Amy Gutmann (ed.) *Multiculturalism and the 'Politics of Recognition'*, Princeton, NJ: Princeton University Press.

Taylor, Charles (1997) 'Nationalism and Modernity', in J. McMahan and R. McKim (eds), *The Ethics of Nationalism*, Oxford: Oxford University Press.

Tully, James (1995) *Strange Multiplicity: Constitutionalism in an Age of Diversity*, Cambridge: Cambridge University Press.

Van Dyke, Vernon (1977) 'The Individual, the State, and Ethnic Communities in Political Theory', *World Politics* 29/3, pp. 343–69.

Van Dyke, Vernon (1982) 'Collective Rights and Moral Rights: Problems in Liberal-Democratic Thought', *Journal of Politics* 44, pp. 21–40.

Van Dyke, Vernon (1985) *Human Rights, Ethnicity and Discrimination*, Westport, Conn.: Greenwood.

van Willigenburg, Theo Robert Heeger and Wilbren van der Burg (eds) (1995) *Nation, State, and the Coexistence of Different Communities*, Kampen, Holland: Kok Pharos.

Walzer, Michael (1992) 'Comment', in Amy Gutmann (ed.) *Multiculturalism and the 'Politics of Recognition'*, Princeton, NJ: Princeton University Press.

Walzer, Michael (1997) *On Toleration*, New Haven, Conn.: Yale University Press.

Ward, Cynthia (1991) 'The Limits of "Liberal Republicanism": Why Group-Based Remedies and Republican Citizenship Don't Mix', *Columbia Law Review* 91/3, pp. 581–607.

Young, Iris Marion (1990) *Justice and the Politics of Difference*, Princeton, NJ: Princeton University Press.

# 3 Nations without states:

## Minority nationalism in the global era

*Michael Keating*

### Analysing nationalism

The resurgence of nationalism in European societies in the late twentieth century has revived all the old debates about its nature, its causes and its effects. There is a bewildering varieties of such theories but all share certain characteristics. They tend to aim at grand or universal explanations of a phenomenon so variegated as often to defy definition. Consequently, theories developed in one context often do not work elsewhere. There is a strong tendency to teleology, as though all social processes were headed in the same direction, whether to the consolidation of the nation-state or to its supercession. There was until recently an assumption that nationalist movements by definition must be seeking their own state. Finally, there is often a strong normative element in the discussion of the classic nineteenth-century nation-state, seen as the essential basis for international order, democracy and social integration. The approach adopted in this chapter is rather different.

It takes the relationship among identity, territory, function and institutions as contingent and changeable (Keating 1988, 1996, 1998). Nations and states are continually being built and rebuilt; history is not just the past but something that we are living now. I do not propose here to get into the well-worn debate between primordialists and instrumentalists. Both are, to a certain point, correct. Nations are 'inventions' but only if we bear in mind the ambiguity of this word. Nowadays, it implies a fabrication, and is used in a pejorative sense to imply that nations and national traditions are mere contrivances (Hobsbawm and Ranger 1983). In its original Latin form, it implies the discovery of something that is already there.[1] The invention of nations lies somewhere between these two, a construction but built upon historical materials which may be more or less manipulated to suit the task.

This picks up on the work of scholars who have explored the problematic nature of the task and the difficulty of incorporating peripheries (Lipset and Rokkan 1967; Rokkan and Urwin 1982, 1983; Tilly 1975), as well as more recent work on the contingent and reversible nature of nation-building processes (Keating 1988; Tilly 1990; Tilly and Blockmans 1994; Spruyt 1994).

The tendency to associate nationalism with the state still perists widely (Hobsbawm 1990). Other scholars have now relaxed this definitional assumption (Smith 1991; Breuilly 1985), conceding that nationalists might aim at something less. Indeed, if we insist that nationalism is about creating one's own state, then we must confine it to the period of the classic nation-state, as Hobsbawm effectively does, or else stretch our definition of the state to the point at which it loses much of its meaning. There are many examples of things that look very like nationalism before the rise of the nation-state as we know it; and nationalism seems as vigorous as ever in an era in which the nation-state is going through a fundamental transition.

On the normative dimension, there is still a tendency for scholars like Dahrendorf (1995) and Hobsbawm (1992) to identify the large nation-state with liberalism, democracy and tolerance and to regard minority nationalism as, by definition, backward and intolerant. This is a lingering metropolitan prejudice which needs to be abandoned if we are to take both minority and majority nationalism seriously.

We are living in a world in which the state, while by no means disappearing, is being transformed in important ways. The relationships between territory, identity, function and institutions are changing. This is providing opportunities for the construction of new systems of social regulation and collective action below and beyond the state but these new systems take a variety of forms. One of these is revived minority nationalisms in those territories where there is a historic sense of identity, an institutional legacy and a political leadership able to construct a new system. This is the process I have elsewhere (Keating 1997) called stateless nation-building.

## The transformation of the state

There is a vigorous debate on whether the nation-state is declining, retreating or being 'hollowed out'. It would exceed the limits of this chapter to deal with this issue in its entirety, but it is evident that the relationships among identity, territory, function and institutions are changing in important ways. The idea of the state has been with us a long time, but the nation-state, in the form in which we know it, is a rather recent phenomenon. It represents the coincidence in space of a number of principles of social and economic organisation. It is the primary focus of collective identity, reinforced and transmitted through culture and socialisation. This collective identity in turn provides the basis for social solidarity. The state is the framework for internal and external security. It frames an economic system, allowing us to talk of national economies, with definable, if not impermeable, boundaries. It is a set of institutions and a mechanism for policy making. In this sense, the nation-state is the product of the modern era and is currently undergoing substantial transformations (Camilleri and Falk 1992). It is transformed institutionally from above, by the rise of transnational regimes, in Europe the European Union and other pan-European bodies; and in North America with the North American Free Trade Agreement (NAFTA); laterally by privatisation and deregulation; and below by territorial assertion. Its functional capacity remains high, but interdependence is limiting its autonomous use of this. Its capacity for economic management is being eroded from above, by global-isation, capital mobility and the rise of the multinational corporation; laterally by the advance of the market; and from below by forms of economic restructuring rooted in local and regional specificities. The three-directional erosion of the nation-state from above, from below, and laterally in the face of the market, has broken the link between economic change and policy making and between policy making and representation. It has undermined social solidarity and made difficult the old class compromises and trade-offs which underpinned the welfare settlement of the postwar era. It has weakened the capacity of states to manage their spatial economies. It has even threatened economic efficiency, by militating against the production of public goods and the social cooperation which is the essential counterpart to competition in a market economy. Power has disappeared into net-works that correspond ever less with the institutional form of the state and mechanisms for democratic representation and deliberation (Castells 1997). The demystification of the state has undermined its legitimacy as the ultimate bearer of values and authority.

So we are in a world where multiple spheres of authority coexist with multiple systems of action. It would be a serious error to present this as totally new, or to contrast it with a mythical state of the classical era which was able to monopolise authority and internalise the policy process. Similarly we should not exaggerate the decline of the state, which still possesses a formidable arsenal of powers and resources. It would also be wrong to assume that the state will disappear merely because it is functionally redundant (even assuming that it is). Powerful public and private interests still have a large investment in the state and it has a strong dynamic of its own. So to imagine that a new state order, based on regions or stateless nations, is about to emerge to replace the European state system, in the way that states emerged from the Roman Empire or the central empires of Europe after 1918, is fundamentally to misinterpret what is happening. The task is much more difficult than this. It is to understand the conditions for building nations as systems of social regulation and collective action in a world where the classical nation-state model is no longer available.

Nationality and nationalism cannot be seen merely as an instrumental doctrine and programme, explained and justified by reference to the functions they perform. Nonetheless, nationality does fulfil social roles (Miller 1995), some of which cannot easily be imagined in its absence. Similarly, the rise of minority nationalism in contemporary society can be seen as an effort to reconstitute the public domain and resolve collective action problems in the face of global markets, social individualism and the crisis of the state. It may be an effort to reconstitute a domain of democratic deliberation and decision in a baffling world of networks and hidden power. We do not therefore have to see it as evidence of lapse into tribalism and the rejection of modernity, nor as evidence of postmodernity. Instead, it can be seen as part of the condition of modernity itself. I emphasise here the 'may' since, like other nationalisms, this form can be xenophobic and demagogic, seeking to blame foreigners and minorities for complex problems. All I am arguing is that we should treat it on the same moral plane as its large-state rivals, whether these rivals consciously express themselves as nationalisms or try and portray themselves in the guise of universalism. In contemporary conditions, we cannot re-establish a public domain by recreating a lost state form, just at a smaller scale and minority nationalisms that seek to do this are doomed to disappointment (Castells 1997) unless they realise the limitations of power. In fact, most of them in developed Western democracies are well aware of this, and seek new forms of public action in the context of global markets and supranational regimes.

## Stateless nation-building

Four states in which the effects of globalisation and supranational integration have combined with the reawakening of minority nationalisms are the United Kingdom, Spain, Belgium and Canada. All of them are sites, not of one challenge to the state, but of several, which take different forms, have different objectives and serve different roles. Nonetheless, they provide material for a systematic comparison of the process of 'stateless nation-building', the construction of new or revalidated imagined communities (Anderson 1983) and of systems of collective action. To a greater or lesser degree these recognise both the limitations of the traditional concept of sovereignty in modern conditions, and the difficulties of confronting established democratic states, which, however functionally weakened, still have such a reservoir of power and legitimacy. In the absence of a state or even a project to create one, these nationalisms need other ways to foster collective identity, to build institutions and to enhance policy capacity. Operating in global markets and free-trade regimes, they need to be at once inward-looking, to foster solidarity, and outward-looking, to operate in the wider trading order.

## Identity

The first requirement is the construction of collective identities. Here we confront the dilemma of modernity (Touraine 1992). A collective identity rooted merely in the past (whether a real or fictive past) provides no basis for coping with the present and future (Renaut 1991). A collective identity based purely on present considerations lacks a basis for values. This is why nationalism cannot be seen merely as instrumentalism. This would not explain how the identity came into being, or why that particular one was chosen. Successful and modernising nationalisms must rather link past and future. So nationalist movements continue to emphasise the past, portraying the nation as ancient and history as a constant struggle for its rights, although the emphasis varies. Quebec nationalists hark back to the conquest by the British in the eighteenth century. Catalans set great store on their existence as a self-governing trading nation before 1714, as do Scots on their former statehood. Basque nationalists claim that the ancient *fueros* are the basis for their claims, not the Spanish constitution. This is not always easy. Sabino de Arana invented a great deal of Basque history to suit his purposes as Basque nationalism, as opposed to mere particularism, was founded at the end of the nineteenth century. Flanders, as we now know it, is a modern creation, not corresponding to any historic unit (Kerremans 1997), excluding much of historic Flanders and including other areas, yet it also seeks a historical legitimation.

If history is important in defining the nation and its claims, this might imply that only natives and their descendants can join in. Yet an identity based purely on ascriptive ('ethnic') criteria not only is questionable on ethical grounds, but also militates against social cooperation and solidarity. A more secure base is cultural identity, where the territorial culture is sufficiently open to assimilate incomers and members of minority groups. This is a delicate issue. A culture which has no common principles fails to provide the basis for solidarity and collective action or citizenship rights. On the other hand, a common culture defined too restrictively may exclude some members of the society and become a mere mark of ethnic differentiation. So culture must be capable of adaptation and absorption of incomers. This implies that immigrants can adopt not only the culture of the society but its history as well.

One of the most frequent criticisms of minority nationalism is that it is discriminatory and even racist, directed against members of the state majority and against immigrants. Often this is based on no more than an assumption, overlooking the exclusive features of the state nationalism itself. Empirical investigation shows a more mixed picture. Basque nationalism was originally highly exclusive, based on blood descent and hostile to incomers. In the course of the twentieth century, however, it has become more inclusive and now officially recognises as Basque all who live in the Basque Country and wish to be Basque. Catalan and Scottish nationalism have been more accommodating and now also explicitly recognise that all can join the nation. The case of Flanders is more difficult, since the nation was built upon the separation of two language groups in a society in which language became the marker of ethnic differentiation, and there has been no attempt to incorporate non-European immigrants. The *Vlaams Blok* is explicitly racist and anti-immigrant and, as with the French National Front, it has been able to set the terms of debate with a frequency out of proportion to its numbers. Quebec nationalism has moved from a narrow concern with 'old stock' Quebeckers (the *Québécois de souche*) to an open nationalism which in principle includes the anglophones and immigrants, but this remains a contentious matter and nationalist activists regularly embarrass the leadership with statements implying the contrary.

Linguistic policy has focused this issue in those cases where there is a distinct language. Enforcing unilingualism may be seen as a mechanism for ethnic exclusion, aimed at all those outside of the core group; or it may be an assimilating measure, preventing outsiders from being ghettoised. Linguistic pluralism may, correspondingly, be seen as a measure of liberal tolerance, or as a way of maintaining the cohesiveness of the core group and marginalising incomers and those who do not speak the language. Quebec's policy has moved from maintaining the cohesion of the francophones through language, to a vigorous effort to integrate newcomers through language, hence the requirement that immigrant children must be educated in French. The local anglophone community, however, are exempt from this requirement. More controversially, it limited public expression in the medium of English through its sign laws. Most of the population are monolingual and the language barrier is the main marker of differentiation, although increasing numbers, especially in the anglophone community, are competent in both languages. Catalonia's language laws are less constraining. They effectively require education in Catalan, but recognise that the society as a whole should be bilingual by requiring all children to be competent in both languages. In the Basque Country, as in Wales, the language is spoken only by a minority. Here policy has been to promote the language through education, broadcasting and culture, extending knowledge and use, while recognising that most people do not function in it. In both cases, there has been a revalorisation of the language, with middle class parents in the cities, whose families are not Basque or Welsh speaking, sending their children to Basque or Welsh schools. In this way, the language becomes part of the nation-building project, a symbol of national identity, even where most people do not speak it. Flanders, on the other hand, is unilingual, the boundaries of the region being so drawn, and even in Brussels the Flemish population come under the authority of the Flanders government for matters connected with language, culture and education. Many Flemish are bilingual but, with the internalisation of public life within Flanders, the second language is increasingly English rather than French.

In general then, stateless nations are using language policy, not to enforce a single cultural code in the manner of nineteenth-century nation-building, but to foster national identity while allowing bilingualism and a degree of pluralism. This open form of nationalism cannot, in general, be considered as a form of discrimination or cultural exclusion. Rather it is a way of permitting the incorporation of outsiders into the nation and should be measured according to its success in this. Only in Flanders, of the cases considered here, is a policy of unilingualism practised, a result of the Belgian decision to resolve linguistic conflict by the effective segregation of the populations.

Corresponding to this greater linguistic sensitivity is a growth in multiple identity, allowing people to feel simultaneously members of the minority nation, of the state nation, and, in come cases, of Europe as well. There is a tendency in all cases for those born in the minority nation and those who speak its language to feel more exclusively members of that nation, while incomers are more likely to feel exclusively of the state nation. Yet nearly all surveys show a majority expressing dual identity, albeit leaning more strongly to one than to the other. Where the cost of assimilation is low, as in Scotland (where there is no language requirement) or Catalonia (where the language is rather easy to learn) large proportions of incomers are assimilated. Fewer are assimilated in the Basque Country or Wales, which remain somewhat divided societies. In Quebec, evidence on the assimilation of incomers is mixed, while there is a stark division in national identity between native francophones and anglophones. The growth of multiple identities is a basic factor allowing these emerging national communities, and actors within them, to operate at multiple levels of action, from the local through the state to the continental level.

## Constitutional options

All the new minority nationalisms make claims about self-determination, claiming the right to negotiate their own constitutional future. Yet the implications of this are far from clear. Some favour independence in the classic sense, at least in the long run. The Scottish National Party (SNP) seeks independence, the *Parti Québécois* (PQ) seeks the 'sovereignty' of Quebec while the Basque Nationalist Party (PNV) more ambiguously favours an independent Basque Country. Yet even in these cases, independence is surrounded by conditions. The SNP combine it with support for advanced European integration, while the PNV see more European integration and the erosion of the state as the precondition for Basque independence. The PQ are divided. Some, like former leader Jacques Parizeau, believe that NAFTA and globalisation will provide all the external support needed for an independent Quebec. Others want to negotiate an additional, bilateral partnership with Canada. Yet even Parizeau wants to free-ride on the Canadian dollar. For the referendum of 1995, there was a compromise in which Quebec was to become sovereign after proposing to Canada an extensive partnership including an economic and monetary union, dual citizenship, joint parliamentary and executive institutions and common positions in international organisations. A large section of public opinion in Quebec seeks a renewed confederation with Canada, in which Quebec's nationality and distinctiveness would be recognised, a position which, in its more advanced forms, meets the moderate wing of the PQ, with its emphasis on partnership with Canada. A similar shading of positions exists in Scotland. While the SNP policy is unambiguously separatist, it is at pains to emphasise the links with Europe and even the inevitability of a 'social union' with England. The Scottish Constitutional Convention, led by the Labour and Liberal Democrat parties and within the home rule, rather than the separatist tradition, insisted on the sovereignty of the Scottish people and its right to renegotiate the union with England. The Labour Party subsequently rejected this position, but their signature on the document remains. The Welsh nationalists in *Plaid Cymru* preach a non-statist form of nationalism which will receive its full expression in a united Europe of the peoples. Catalonia's *Convergència i Unió* insist on the inherent rights of Catalonia to nego-tiate with Spain but are equally insistent that Catalonia's future will be within a Spanish confederation and not as a nation-state. The *Esquerra Republicana de Catalunya* are more clearly independentist but insist that this is only for the long term, in the context of a Europe in which nation states have disappeared altogether. The Flemish parties are similarly divided and ambiguous. The *Vlaams Blok* preaches an old-fashioned nationalism, but draws its support from its racist and anti-immigrant stance. The *Volksunie* shares the ambiguity of other European nationalists. It favours independence but is ready to wait for the collapse of the Belgian state to permit Flanders to become inde-pendent in Europe. The Christian Democrats pursue an even more ambiguous line whose end state would appear to be an independent Flanders in an integrated Europe, without explicitly stating this.

   This ambivalence might be considered mere opportunism, but it does reflect the genuine uncertainty over the meaning of independence and self-government in the modern world. It also finds its echo in public opinion. Surveys consistently show a significant number of Québécois in favour of sovereignty and even independence, while also wanting to remain within Canada. A similar phenomenon is found in Catalonia, where responses to 'soft questions' about whether people feel positively about the independence of Catalonia get much higher support than 'hard' questions on separatism. In Scotland a similar ambivalence is often found. It is tempting to put this down to public ignorance about constitutional matters and the categories employed. It could be argued, on the other hand, that the public is showing a realistic appreciation of the ambiguity of these categories in the modern world.

### The transnational dimension

All the minority nationalist movements now set their demands in the context of globalisation and the rise of transnational regimes, notably the EU and NAFTA. For some, this is merely an instrumental use, a way of showing that the costs of independence are lowered and that, in an interdependent world, the state would have an interest in maintaining trading links and cooperation with a seceding nation. This is more or less the position of former PQ leader Jacques Parizeau, who argues that NAFTA and other international agreements would allow Quebec to dispense with a special partnership with Canada. The SNP usually take a similar line with regard to Scottish membership of the EU, with rather more credibility since the EU has much stronger common institutions than NAFTA, especially with the single currency. More often, however, minority nationalists use globalisation and transnational regimes as a way of sustaining their case for a non-separatist form of nationalism. There are various ways in which the emerging European and transnational order can accommodate territorial nationalisms. One is by lowering the costs of independence and making the transition to it easier. It may be that the dissolution of the Belgian state will be both hastened and smoothed by European integration, since Europe will look after key functions like trade, economic regulation, monetary policy and (as Europe or via the North Atlantic Treaty Organisation – NATO) defence. It is unlikely, however, that European states will willingly contemplate their dismemberment within Europe and secession remains a grave step, even within a transnational order. More interesting, perhaps, is the way in which Europe allows an unpacking of the idea of sovereignty and creates a new arena in which nationalities can express themselves. The very nature of the EU involves rethinking sovereignty, although not all states have been willing to accept this; and other pan-European bodies like the Council of Europe further challenge the monopoly of the state. More specifically, Europe performs three roles.

First, it allows human and civil rights to be detached from the state, principally through the Council of Europe and its human rights machinery. This removes the pretension that only the nation-state can guarantee equal rights and allows these to be expressed in more genuinely universal terms, without the nationalist connotations implied in their being the property of the nation-state. It is notable that the main objection of Quebec nationalists to the Canadian Charter of Rights is not the detailed content, which is very similar to that of Quebec's own charter, but the fact that it was used as an instrument of Canadian nation-building in a project that denied the specificity of Quebec. North America, however, lacks a transnational rights system comparable to that of Europe. The European Convention on Human Rights, on the other hand, has been used extensively in the UK to entrench rights under devolution. In the Northern Ireland peace agreement, it is laid down that acts of the Northern Ireland Assembly will be subject directly to the European Convention on Human Rights, so ensuring that rights will not be tainted by being seen as the emanation of either Irish or British justice. The Scottish devolution settlement contains similar provisions. Europe, this time through the EU, also stipulates equality of treatment in various economic and social matters. Since these provisions are binding equally on state and non-state entities, they are more acceptable to minority nations. The condition of all this, it must be noted, is that Europe should not strive to be a state itself, nor to foster a European nationality, but remain as a neutral political space, informed by universal conceptions of human rights and justice, but without the ambition to become a nation. Were it to do so, it would merely recreate the old problems of associating civil and human rights with a specific nation-building project, and risk provoking opposition both from existing states and stateless nations.

Second, Europe provides a range of opportunities for functional autonomy for stateless nations. The Europe of the Regions argument was over-stated in the early 1990s and there is no clear structure for the representation of stateless nations in the institutions of the EU. There are, however, myriad opportunities through lobbying in Brussels, inter-regional networks, consultative committees and partnerships in European regional policy (Jáuregui 1997; Petschen 1993; Bullman 1994; Jones and Keating 1995). It is not possible to use European institutions to bypass or confront state governments, since the states remain the prime actors in the EU. The most successful regions and stateless nations are the ones that use multiple channels of access, including their own state governments, recognising the complexity of policy networks and the diffusion of power and authority. Success also depends on the powers that regions and stateless nations are given to operate within Europe and internationally. The Belgian regions and communities have full external competence corresponding to their domestic competences and have been able to act directly in Europe in a number of ways. In other states, including Spain, central governments have been at pains to restrict the international activities of sub-state actors, although both Catalonia and the Basque Country have been very active in the Europe of the Regions movement, with offices in Brussels and an extensive network of international contacts. The UK devolution legislation provides specifically for a Scottish role in the EU, including a representative office in Brussels.

Third, and perhaps more importantly, Europe provides a new discursive space for minority nationalists, providing multiple opportunities for symbolic projection as more than mere regions. Operating at the

European and international level in turn helps nation-building at home, legitimising the project and giving it the external and international dimension so important to nationhood. It is this, above all, that explains the strong pro-Europeanism of most minority nationalists in the European Union. Again, the precondition is that Europe not be a state but rather be a structured arena, providing opportunities for actors of different types. The symbolic content of nationalism is often underestimated or dismissed as irrelevant or as a form of false consciousness. Yet where nationality and nationalism are defined as claims to a reference group, to a space and to self-determination, symbolic issues take on great importance. Indeed, the debate on Quebec's place in Canada has come down to a debate about symbolism and recognition. The Meech Lake Accord foundered essentially on the unwillingness of Canada outside Quebec to accept such a weak formulation of this as the declaration that Quebec was a 'distinct society'. Europe provides a forum in which all manner of symbolic nationality claims can be staked, from the presence of 'embassies' in Brussels, to the travels of regional presidents, to the practice of flying three flags, the European, the state and the regional/national one. There is evidence that the effort to place the minority national identity in a European context is working. Catalans have become notably more pro-European in the 1980s and 1990s, adding this to their repertoire of multiple identities. Basques are more particularist, but they too have become more Europeanised (García Ferrando *et al.* 1994; Sangrador García 1996; Moral 1998). Scottish public opinion is more favourable to Europe than that of other parts of the United Kingdom, a reversal of the position in the 1970s and which reflects the instrumentalisation of Europe both by the Labour movement and the Scottish nationalist movement (Brown *et al.* 1998). A parallel phenomenon is visible in Canada, where Quebec has consistently been more favourable to free trade than other regions (Martin 1997).

The EU is not the only such space in which minority nations can gain recognition. There is the Council of Europe, which has been active in the promotion of minority languages and cultures, and there are other European forums. The Francophonie provides a platform for Quebec, alongside Canada. Many national minorities argue that UNESCO should not just represent states, but should include all entities with their own cultural and educational institutions. Given that Scotland, for example, has its own educational system quite separate from that of England, and now subject to separate political control, it is argued that there is no particular reason why the Scots should have to share a delegation with the English, Welsh and Northern Irish. This argument has been made in the Basque Country and Catalonia and is a live issue in Belgium. Under the Northern Ireland peace agreement, multiple forums are created to diffuse sovereignty, including the British–Irish Council, a body that includes a whole range of sovereign, non-sovereign and semi-sovereign entities, including the British and Irish states, the Scottish Parliament, the Welsh and Northern Ireland assemblies, the Isle of Man and the Channel Islands.

This attitude is not merely the product of material self-interest and, indeed, the embrace of free trade regimes may be a source of contradiction and conflict with nationalist coalitions. Quebec trade unions have supported sovereignty within NAFTA as nationalists, while opposing NAFTA as trade unionists. Quebec farmers have supported sovereignty, despite the fact that being exposed directly to NAFTA rules would be devastating for most of them. Scottish and Basque nationalists are enthusiasts for the EU, although opposed to many of its policies in such important fields as fisheries, agriculture and competition. Nor do all minority nationalists share the same vision of the transnational regime. The SNP favours an intergovernmental EU, with power firmly in the hands of member states. *Convergència i Unió* is much more supportive of a supranational Europe, which would weaken the Spanish framework without the need for secession. *Plaid Cymu* and the *Esquerra Republicana de Catalunya* are more utopian, looking for a new Europe in which old fashioned states disappear altogether. Within the main nationalist parties of Spain, there are sharp differences among the PNV, who seek ultimate Basque independence in Europe, CiU, who prefer to reconstruct the Spanish state on a plurinational basis, and the *Bloque Nacionalista Galego*, which retains a residual but strong suspicion of Europe. These three were able to issue a series of common declarations in 1998, starting with that of Barcelona, but these barely disguised the differences in their approach.

### Developmental nationalism

The abandonment of the old state form and the embrace of free trade and globalisation face the new minority nationalisms with the problem of inserting their economies in the new trading order without subjecting themselves entirely to it. With the weakening of the capacity of the state to engage in macroeconomic management in the face of global trends, emphasis has shifted to microeconomic policy, innovation, entrepreneurship and training. A growing body of literature has traced the importance of territorial systems of production, located at the local or regional level and able to foster a balance between competition and cooperation, encouraging the production of goods and positive externalities (Storper 1997). The rather vague term 'social capital' has come to be used to describe the potential for problem solving and social cooperation in territorial societies. This is a key element in the 'new regionalism' (Keating 1998) which seeks to build regions as systems of social regulation and collective action below and alongside the nation state, focused on the needs of development in a globalised economy.

This type of developmental regionalism and minority nationalism are in many cases complementary. Nationalism provides the rationale for social cooperation and promoting a territorial economic model has become an integral part of nation-building. The best known example is from Quebec where, in the course of the Quiet Revolution, an indigenous business class was fostered, with an interventionist state, and quasi-corporatist connections among government, business and unions (Latouche 1991). Rather misleadingly and exaggeratedly labelled 'Quebec Inc.', this was a form of developmental nationalism intended first to recover control of the economy from Canadian anglophone interests and then to manage Quebec's insertion into the North American and global trading order. Questions have now been raised about this model, especially about the effects of globalisation and internationalisation of Quebec firms on the cohesion of the development coalition. Other critics complain that the move to neo-liberal policies by successive Quebec governments, Liberal and PQ, has undermined the model. Its defenders, on the other hand, argue that it is precisely in the conditions of globalisation that this kind of cohesion is most valuable. Flanders has rather consciously imitated this pattern, fostering small Flemish firms, in a context marked by the decline of the old Walloon heavy industries. It has the advantage that broader economic trends have favoured Flanders, restoring its historic role as a centre of European trade.

The Basque Country has been active in industrial policy, exploiting both the flexibility of its special tax system, and the networks of cooperation among Basque entrepreneurs. In Catalonia, policy has been less interventionist, but the theme of promoting Catalonia in European markets has been a leitmotif for social cooperation and steering. The historical model of Catalonia as a medieval trading nation has served as a mobilising myth for nation-building in modern conditions. Welsh identity has to some extent been reforged, with the emphasis on Wales as a European economic region rather than just the language issue. A great deal of effort has been put into trying to demonstrate the aptness of Welsh traditions of social cooperation and solidarity for the needs of the 'learning region'. This adaptation of Welshness to current conditions is one explanation for the victory, albeit narrow, in the 1997 referendum on devolution, compared with the overwhelming defeat in 1979. In Scotland, developmental regionalism has a long history. Efforts at economic regeneration, going back to the 1960s, were an important factor in strengthening a sense of Scottish identity and giving it a contemporary economic meaning. This programme was managed before 1999, not by nationalists but by decentralised arms of the British state, yet it served to strengthen Scottish identity and has been transformed into a form of developmental nationalism.

## Institution building

Finally, there is the dimension of institution-building. Stateless nations have benefited from the functionally driven tendency to decentralisation and regionalisation across Western countries since the late 1960s (Keating 1998). Even a state which long resisted political decentralisation, like the United Kingdom, has been forced to build regional institutions for administration and social dialogue. It also used administrative devolution, in Scotland and Wales, as a means of staving off demands for political devolution, a strategy which backfired since the effect of administrative decentralisation was to enhance the relevance of Scotland and Wales as governmental units and to make them into political arenas. In Spain, Canada and Belgium, political devolution has been conceded as a response to minority nationalist demands, a strategy extended more recently to the UK. At the same time, there is a tendency for the institutions of civil society, including business associations, trade unions, cultural and social bodies, to strengthen their distinctiveness within the minority nation, further consolidating the sense of national identity.

Since nation-building is a very uneven process, this has led to demands for asymmetrical concessions and, in varying degrees, to asymmetrical government. The Spanish constitution of 1978 allows asymmetry by permitting, but not requiring, all regions to establish autonomous communities and providing both fast and slow tracks. Spanish governments have consistently sought to keep the process symmetrical by holding back the strong regions and encouraging the weak but the process of institutionalisation, whatever the legalities, is more advanced in the three historic nationalities and Navarre. The Canadian debate has similarly been polarised between those who favour and those who oppose a special recognition of Quebec (McRoberts 1997) but, de facto, Quebec has assumed many of the roles of a national government, while other provinces have not. Its civil society is also very distinct. The Belgian constitution is highly complex, with its provisions for both territorial and community-based devolution. In practice it is asymmetrical since the Flemish government and parliament have merged and achieved a higher degree of institutional coherence than their Walloon/Francophone counterparts. Brussels is managed by a further tier of complexity involving both community governments and its own regional government. In the UK, civil society has always been highly differentiated, especially between England and Wales on the one hand, and Scotland on the other. Since 1999 this is reflected in the constitutional arrangements, which provide for a legislative Scottish Parliament and an administrative Welsh Assembly, while England remains under the direct control of the Westminster Parliament and Whitehall ministries. The Northern Ireland Good Friday peace agreement provides for a highly complex and asymmetrical arrangement, treating the province as a problem *sui generis* and allowing its citizens to identify with either or both neighbouring states.

## The evolving state

The new and re-emerging minority nationalisms are uneven in their impact and varied in their content and demands. So there is no new model emerging to replace the classic nation-state. Rather we see a plurality of movements seeking to carve out a space in the emerging state and international order. State responses to this process vary greatly, but two are of particular interest here, that of further functional decentralisation to give minority nations more power and, much more difficult, a symbolic reconstruction of the state and nation to recognise the principle of multiple identity, and multiple nationalities.

Functional decentralisation can accommodate many of the substantive demands of minority nationalists. Language and cultural policy can be decentralised and territorialised, as has happened in all four states considered here. Development policy can be decentralised according to the functional logic of the new regional development thinking. Other issues can be passed upwards to transnational regimes. Yet territorial decentralisation does not solve all problems and in the case of divided societies there may be a need for further unpacking of sovereignty and devolution to cultural communities. Indeed, beyond a certain point, functional decentralisation may end up destroying the state altogether, as in happening in Belgium, for two reasons.

As functions are transferred down to the regions and communities and up to the EU, the state is also becoming functionally redundant, remaining in being in order to manage common problems, like the question of Brussels, rather than to express a national will. At the same time, as elites based in the regions and communities have taken over the national political system, they destroy the idea of a Belgian political class. It is not clear that a state can survive as a mere holding company for functions that cannot be transferred elsewhere or that nobody wants.

In Canada, Quebec nationalism confronts a Canadian nation-building project of approximately the same vintage, neither of which can easily make the symbolic concessions to the other required for coexistence. It is this symbolic domain, rather than issues of functional decentralisation, that has caused the impasse on the Quebec–Canada question. Similarly, in Spain, there is a division between those who are prepared to devolve competences in a symmetrical manner to all autonomous communities, thus giving Catalonia, the Basque Country and Galicia more effective power, and those who see the issue as involving the very character of the state, as a uniform nation-state or as a plurinational confederation. The constitution of 1978 fudges the issue by speaking of the indissoluble unity of the Spanish nation but also of the nationalities and regions that compose it. An understanding that the term nationalities was a recognition of the special status of Catalonia, the Basque Country and Galicia was undermined when the term was extended to Aragon and the Canaries. As already mentioned, the Labour Party signed on to the declaration of Scottish sovereignty in the Constitutional Convention then, in government, insisted that Scottish devolution in no way abrogated the sovereignty of Parliament. These issues are not merely semantic. Underlying the symbolic recognition of nationality is the implication that a nation, as opposed to a mere region, does have certain intrinsic rights of self-determination which, while not necessarily giving a right of unilateral secession, do give the nation a right to negotiate its position within the state.

There is still a great unwillingness to recognise the category of stateless nation as a stable or viable form. Many social scientists insist that nationalism must be about getting a state and that, if nationalists deny this, it is mere subterfuge. Usually, this is rooted in the 'realist' assumption that nationalists will maximise their power and influence through secession. Yet there is an equally plausible case to be made that nationalists as rational actors will in certain circumstances avoid separatism as being too costly and as provoking resistance not only to separatism itself but to most of their moderate claims as well. Among Catalan nationalists there is a strong view that the best way to promote autonomy and nation-building is precisely by not talking of secession or even thinking of it (Puig 1998).

Many minority nationalists themselves still cling to the state model as the only generally accepted recognition of nationhood even when, as we have seen, they surround it with qualifications. State elites themselves, especially in the majority communities, have also tended to this view, equating the right of self-determination with that of secession. This was illustrated by the Canadian government's reference to the Supreme Court of the issue of whether Quebec had the right unilaterally to secede. The Court satisfied hardliners on both sides by saying that it did, but only under very difficult conditions. What it did not address was the question really posed by successive constitutional negotiations, that of whether Quebec had the right to self-determination and to negotiate a new position within the Canadian fold. By insisting that states must be nations, and nations must be states, state leaders are ironically encouraging secessionist tendencies (Jáuregui 1997). It is now reasonably clear, for example, that a large part of the YES vote in the 1995 Quebec referendum came from people who did not want independence but did want to assert Quebec's right to negotiate its status. Such voters are continually frustrated by Canadian and Quebec nationalists who insist that the only options are independence or being a province like the others. Ironically, the United Kingdom which, until recently, had conceded less functional devolution than the other cases, has long been ready to make these symbolic concessions. Irish and Scottish unionists in the nineteenth century argued, not that their societies were not nations but that, as nations, their future was better secured within the United Kingdom. Yet in another sense they drew the same conclusions, that Scotland and Ireland being nations would use their symbolic capital to challenge the United Kingdom and the doctrine of parliamentary sovereignty. Now the UK government has conceded Home Rule, in different ways, to Scotland and Wales and launched an open-ended process of transfer of powers to Northern Ireland. It continues to repeat that none of this abridges the principle of parliamentary sovereignty but, when combined with further European integration, this becomes more and more of an empty slogan.

We are therefore entering an era of diffused sovereignty and complex government, in which certain territorial minorities are able to invoke the principle of nationality, recast for the global era, to advance claims to self-government and build systems of action in state and civil society. The implications are another topic, which would go beyond the scope of this chapter (Keating 1999a, 1999b). The future seems to be for an increasingly asymmetrical state system embedded in asymmetrical supranational orders, notably in Europe, to reconcile the conflicting claims of nationality and self-determination. The very flexibility of such a system is, in the view of critics, an element of instability since nationalist and other territorial leaders will continually seek to outbid each other. Yet this tendency finds a corrective mechanism in European integration, which has led nationalists to moderate their demands, as well as providing for a new system of regulation above the nation. It is very likely therefore that the process of European integration and the loosening of the state framework will continue to run in parallel. In Canada, where there is no equivalent to the European political order, nationalist politics appear as more of a zero-sum game and the outcome could be more conflictual.

## Note

1  This is the sense in which Oneto (1997) applies the word to Padania.

## References

Anderson, B. (1983), *Imagined Communities: Reflections on the Origins and Spread of Nationalism*, London: Verso.
Breuilly, J. (1985), *Nationalism and the State*, Manchester: Manchester University Press.
Brown, A., D. McCrone and L. Paterson (1998), *Politics and Society in Scotland*, 2nd edn, London: Macmillan.
Bullman, U. (ed.) (1994), *Die Politik der Dritten Ebene*, Baden-Baden: Nomos.
Camilleri, J. and J. Falk (1992), *The End of Sovereignty? The Politics of a Shrinking and Fragmenting World*, Aldershot: Edward Elgar.
Castells, Manuel (1997), *The Information Age: Economy, Society and Culture. Volume 1, The Power of Identity*, Oxford: Blackwell.
Dahrendorf, R. (1995), 'Preserving Prosperity', *New Statesmen and Society*, 13/29 December.
García Ferrando, Manuel, Eduardo López-Aranguren and Miguel Beltrán (1994), *La conciencia nacional y regional en la España de las autonomías*, Madrid: Centro de Investigaciones Sociológicas.
Hobsbawm, E. (1990), *Nations and Nationalism since 1780*, Cambridge: Cambridge University Press.
Hobsbawm, E. (1992), 'Nationalism: Whose Fault-line is it Anyway?', *Anthropology Today*, February.

Hobsbawm, E. and T. Ranger (eds) (1983), *The Invention of Tradition*, Cambridge: Cambridge University Press.

Jáuregui, G. (1997) *Los nacionalismos minoritarios y la Unión Europea*, Barcelona, Ariel.

Jones, B. and M. Keating (eds) (1995), *The European Union and the Regions*, Oxford: Oxford University Press.

Keating, M. (1988), *State and Regional Nationalism: Territorial Politics and the European State*, London: Harvester-Wheatsheaf.

Keating, M. (1996), *Nations against the State: The New Politics of Nationalism in Quebec, Catalonia and Scotland*, London: Macmillan.

Keating, M. (1997), 'Stateless nation-building: Quebec, Catalonia and Scotland in the changing state system', *Nations and Nationalism*, 3.4, pp. 689–717.

Keating, M. (1998), *The New Regionalism in Western Europe: Territorial Restructuring and Political Change*, Aldershot: Edward Elgar.

Keating, M. (1999a), 'Le gouvernement asymétrique: principes et problèmes', *Politique et sociétés* 17.3, pp. 93–111.

Keating, M. (1999b), 'Asymmetrical Government: Multinational States in an Integrating Europe', *Publius: The Journal of Federalism*, 29.1, pp. 71–86.

Kerremans, B. (1997), 'The Flemish Identity: Nascent or Existent?', *Res Publica*, 39.2, pp. 303−14.

Latouche, D. (1991), 'La stratégie québécoise dans le nouvel ordre économique et politique internationale', *Commission sur l'avenir politique et constitutionnel du Québec, Document de travail numéro 4*, Quebec: Commission.

Lipset, S.M and D. Rokkan (1967), *Party Systems and Voter Alignments*, New York: Free Press.

MacCormick, N. (1999), *Questioning Sovereignty: State and Nation in the European Commonwealth*, Oxford: Oxford University Press.

McRoberts, K. (1997), *Misconceiving Canada: The Struggle for National Unity*, Toronto: Oxford University Press.

Martin, P. (1997), 'The Politics of Free Trade in Quebec', in M. Keating and J. Loughlin (eds) *The Political Economy of Regionalism*, London: Frank Cass.

Miller, D. (1995) *On Nationality*, Oxford: Oxford University Press.

Moral, Félix (1998) 'Identidad regional y nacionalismo en el Estado de las autonomías, *Opiniones y Actitudes, 18*, Madrid: Centro de Investigaciones Sociológicas.

Oneto, G. (1997), *L'invenzione della Padania: La rinascita della communità più antica d'Europa*, Ceresola, Spain: Foedus.

Petschen, S. (1993), *La Europa de las regiones*, Barcelona: Generalitat de Catalunya.

Puig i Scotoni, P. (1998), *Pensar els camins a la sobirania*, Barcelona: Mediterrània.

Renaut, A. (1991), 'Logiques de la nation', in G. Delannoi and P-A. Taguieff (eds) *Théories du Nationalisme*, Paris: Kimé.

Rokkan, S. and Urwin, D. W. (1982), *The Politics of Territorial Identity: Studies in European Regionalism*, London: Sage.

Rokkan, S. and Urwin, D. W. (1983), *Economy Territory Identity: Politics of West European Peripheries*, London: Sage.

Sangrador García, José Luis (1996) 'Identidades, actitudes y estereotipos en la España de las Autonomías', *Opiniones y Actitudes, 10*, Madrid: Centro de Investigaciones Sociológicas.

Smith, A. (1991), *National Identity*, London: Penguin.

Spruyt, H. (1994), *The Sovereign State and its Competitors*, Princeton, NJ: Princeton University Press.

Storper, M. (1997), *The Regional World: Territorial Development in a Global Economy*, New York: Guilford.

Tilly, C. (1975), *The Formation of National States in Western Europe*, Princeton, NJ: Princeton University Press.

Tilly, C. (1990) *Coercion, Capital, and European States, AD 990–1990*, Oxford: Basil Blackwell.

Tilly, C. and Blockmans, W. (1994) *Cities and the Rise of States in Europe, AD 1000 to 1800*, Boulder, Col.: Westview Press.

Touraine, A. (1992), *Critique de la modernité*, Paris; Fayard.

# Part II

# National pluralism and democratic institutions

# 4   National plurality and equality

*Enric Fossas*

In this chapter I will be considering various aspects relating to equality in federal states, particularly in those of a multinational character, and I will try to demonstrate that, in spite of the tendency towards homogenisation in the majority of modern federal systems, federalism – even today – still allows for a certain diversity which is not to be found in unitary states. Nevertheless, as I will outline below, the development of federal structures in multinational states is especially difficult and continues, in many ways, to conflict with the idea of equality that has accompanied the nation-state. I will begin by introducing certain conceptual clarifications concerning both the idea of the multinational federal state and the concept of equality. I will follow this with the three aspects of the relationship between multinational federalism and equality under consideration, namely, that which affects the founding groups or peoples in a federation; that which refers to the units integrated within a federal state and that which touches upon the citizens of a federation. I will finish by outlining the conclusions that may be drawn from what will have been discussed.

## Conceptual clarifications

Clearly, if we are to compare federalism and equality we first need to observe some of their characteristic features, since we are dealing with very broad ranging terms that are not possible to define in any precise way. In this sense we could say that we are dealing with two concept-values that have their own tone and which orient themselves in a specific, given direction (Elazar 1987). As with many other political or legal concepts, they are symbolic and combative concepts that have their *ratio* not in the wish for knowledge but rather in their instrumental suitability for controversy with the adversary (García Pelayo

1984: 33). In my opinion, and given these circumstances, the distinction between 'federalism', 'federal political systems' and 'federation' (Watts 1994: 8) seems to be absolutely valid. The first would be a normative concept expressing the idea that political organisation should seek to achieve both political integration and political freedom by combining shared rule on some matters with self-rule on others. The second would be a descriptive term to refer to the genus of political organisation that provides for the combination of shared rule and self-rule (federation, confederation, federacy, unions, leagues). And the third would be specific species within the genus of federal political systems, in concrete, that invented by the founding fathers of the United States at Philadelphia in 1787, and which would later extend itself to countries such as Canada, Australia, Germany, India, Switzerland or Brazil. This specific form is also referred to as a federal state, and, in spite of the variations that can be observed in the form it takes in the various countries where it is applied, there are a series of common characteristics that can be summarised by the following comments: it is a structure and process of governance that establishes unity while preserving diversity by constitutionally uniting separate political communities into a limited, but encompassing, political community in which power is divided and shared between a general government having nationwide responsibilities, and constituent governments having local responsibilities (Kincaid 1991: 392).

From this basis, however, we still need to make two further distinctions: in the first place, we need to distinguish between integrative federalism and devolutionary federalism (Lenaerts 1990: 206). The first designates a constitutional order that strives at unity in diversity among previously independent or confederally related component groups. If need be, the system is fully capable of acknowledging the existence of societal pluralism from one component body to another. The second refers to a constitutional order that redistributes the power of the previously unitary state among its component groups. The principal concern is to organise diversity in unity.

The other distinction is between territorial federalism and multinational federalism (Resnick 1994; Kymlicka 1998). The first type is that which adopts itself as a form of organising power in a wide and diverse territory, independent of the ethnocultural composition of the population, with the aim of providing greater efficiency to the government, greater proximity to power for its citizens, and a greater guarantee of freedom, which is achieved precisely by dividing power territorially. Examples of this kind of arrangement would be the USA, Australia or Germany. The second type is that which aims to accommodate – within the same political space – the diverse national communities that demand recognition of their differentiated identities, and that are making a claim for a level of self-control sufficient to guarantee the maintenance and development of that identity, as is the case in Canada, Belgium and Spain.

Equality can be considered as a general principle in the organisation of the constitutional state because it resides within its very basis, and because it is also a subjective right that is guaranteed to all citizens in a liberal-democratic system. In both these senses, it is a concept which has historically been formulated in many different ways, and continues to be so even today, as can be demonstrated by the fact that the 'equalities' (Sartori 1992: 89) are at the centre of the current debate on justice between moral and political philosophy. In this chapter, I understand equality as a 'relational' concept (Rubio Llorente 1993: 640), that is, a concept which places at least two people, two objects or two situations in some sort of relation, and which makes reference to the treatment or consideration that the public powers exercise on these people, objects or situations. In this sense, we can distinguish between legal equality (by which we refer to that of all citizens before the law and its application); political equality (to indicate that which affects the access to and exercising of public power in a democratic state); and economic equality (to indicate that which makes reference to the equitable distribution of burdens and benefits, which the members of a community support or obtain from public powers).

As I have already indicated, the three equalities that I will be examining are those which refer to the founding groups or peoples of a given federation, to the units which are integrated within a federal state, and to the citizens in the various different ambits mentioned above. At the same time, I will try to highlight the importance that the plurinational character of the federation has in the conception of these three equalities.

## Diversity among founding peoples or subjects

The concept of federalism links the creation of a political body through a pact (*foedus*), to a voluntary association between previously existing and equal subjects or peoples. This model of alliance is in contraposition to two other models: conquest and organic evolution (Elazar 1987). The model of the pact places the emphasis on the union between bodies that are *equal* among themselves, in such a way that once the new political body has been created, all its constituent members maintain the same rights. Nevertheless, if we look at the historical experience of certain federations, the principle of equality among the founding bodies has not always been fully observed.

In the case of the United States, the twelve states that signed the Philadelphia Convention (1787) affirmed the principle of equality among themselves, yet the majority of constituent states pronounced themselves against equality when the discussion centred on the admission of new members to the Union (Madison 1908: 89). Only later, and in spite of not forming part of the constitutional text, was the decision of the Supreme Court to establish the principle of equality among the states '*in power, dignity and authority*' (*Coyle v. Oklahoma (1911)* 221 U.S. 559, 576). The United States represents an example of integrative and territorial federalism: it arose from the union of the thirteen pre-existing colonies, although it is true that none of these was controlled by a national minority, and the division of the powers within the federal system was not designed to accommodate ethnocultural divisions (Kymlicka 1996). As is well known, the nature of this union was the object of argument, and even of conflict: nevertheless, a good number of the founding fathers, such as Hamilton, saw the constitution not only as a regime of liberty, but also and especially as the promise of nationhood (Beer 1994: 4). His supporters, in *The Federalist*, transformed the term 'federal' from what had previously been understood by the word, and described the new system as 'national and at the same time federal'.

Canada was created as a confederation of four British colonies – Nova Scotia, New Brunswick, Lower Canada (Quebec) and Upper Canada (Ontario) – and as a British Dominion by means of the British North America Act of 1876. But, as with the USA, the nature of this constitutional union has been the focus of controversy between several differing points of view (Rocher and Smith 1995: 45). The so-called 'compact theory' sees Canada as the creation of the Provinces maintaining equality among one another and in their relation to the federal government. However, the resulting federation is an irregular and multiform assemblage, since the equality that it embodies is not the identity of political and legal institutions, but rather the equal recognition and autonomy of diverse forms of provincial self-government; and the irregularity of the federation will increase still further as other provinces join (Tully 1995). In contrast to the 'compact theory' is the 'dualist vision' which sees the Confederation as a pact between two founding nations ('*deux peuples fondateurs*'), in reference to the English speaking Protestant majority on the one hand, and to the French speaking Catholic minority on the other. The concept of Canada as a federation of two nationalities on an equal footing gained force at the time of the Quiet Revolution, and has been an underlying part of the demands that Québécois nationalism has made since then. As we will see, this conflict of perspectives is the basis of the Canadian constitutional debate on asymmetric federalism.

In Germany, the imperial Constitution of 1871 was not articulated under the principle of the equality of the states; rather, it was angled towards providing special status for Bavaria, Baden and Württemberg, which were given greater autonomy in relation to other states. Special status was also given to Prussia in view of its demographic and political importance. This included, among other prerogatives, an over-representation in the *Bundesrat*, or upper chamber.

German legal doctrine was particularly interested in the question of equality between the states. Laband (1900) wrote that, in effect, the federal character of Imperial Germany itself was based on the existence of states that were equal in law; but from this situation it was not impossible to confer particular rights to given states, provided that this did not undermine the responsibilities and obligations of other states. These particular rights (*jura singularia*) constituted state rights in relation to the whole, and from the point of view of their content, they could consist of limitations to the power of the Empire (Bavaria), situations of privilege for certain states within the Imperial organisation (Prussia), or fiscal privileges. The common feature of all these rights was that they could not be overridden without the agreement of the state concerned. According to Laband (1900: 185), particular rights (*jura singularia*) should not be confused with the rights of members *as such* (*jura singulorum*), that is to say, with that part of state power exercised by each state, and which did not correspond to the Empire. Germany is an example of a nation-state with a pre-existing political identity. The Germans felt themselves to be a nation before there was a single Germanic State, and they sought to establish political unity within the heart of this state, with the aim thereby of better expressing their national links.

These examples show that the idea of establishing equality between the constituting political bodies within a federal state has not always been roundly accomplished in historical reality. The explanation for this most probably lies in the fact that the first federal organisations (as with others that were not federal) were weighed down by the consequences of 'pactism' and 'contractualism' that were more representative of premodern political systems, characterised by the diversity of forms in the political articulation present within a given territory. The evolution of the modern state has taken place along lines that run in the opposite direction to earlier constitutional asymmetry, basically because of the force of three specific pressures: the innovative and interventionist impulses that characterise the modern state; democratisation and its implications on civil equality; and the Jacobin doctrine of national unity (Keating 1998: 93). The tendency towards unification and uniformity culminated in the phenomenon of the nation-state (Guibernau 1996: 57), to which federalism has aimed at providing a 'counter-voice'. At the close of the twentieth century, the demands for cultural recognition on the part of minority groups, communities and collectives, and (particularly) the claims made by national minorities, have raised questions concerning the constitutional schemes of the nation-state, and have even highlighted the limits of federalism in accommodating plurinational realities. In fact, the debate on equality between federal units has been carried out precisely in these multinational federations, as I will explain in the following section.

## Equality between the units of a multinational federal state

In a now well-known article by Ch. D. Tarlton (1965: 861), the question of equality between the member states of a federation was first raised, albeit in a speculative way. The author criticised several of the main academic writers who had studied federalism, since, to his way of seeing the issue, they had been considering federal systems 'as a whole', accepting that member states shared identical relations with the federal government, whereas in reality it was evident that a system 'may be more or less federal throughout its parts'. According to Tarlton, the fundamentally important aspect of the issue lay in the diverse ways in which each federated unit is able to establish relations with the system as a whole, with the central authority, and with the remaining units. The homogeneity of these relations is precisely what defines a federal system as 'symmetric', while the absence of homogeneity results in an 'asymmetric' system. The fact of a member state relation being symmetric or asymmetric depends on the extent, greater or lesser, to which that state shares the social, cultural, economic and political characteristics of the federal system of which it forms part. Tarlton does not include the possible national character of a member state among these characteristics for the simple reason that his ideas, while theoretical, were nevertheless concerned essentially with US federalism, and, as we have already observed, this is not multinational.

In spite of this reflection, however, in the most important discussions that have subsequently taken place concerning federal asymmetry, the question of national character has become linked to the notion of the plurinational character of the state and, as a result, these discussions have largely taken place in the contexts of states whose national composition has still to be definitively resolved, and which is the object of public debate. Within the framework of Western democracies, the countries that have developed this debate most vigorously are Canada, Spain and Belgium, since in each of these countries there are territorial political units which identify themselves as 'national communities' (Quebec, Flanders, Catalonia and the Basque Country), and which coexist with other units that refer to themselves as 'regions' of the nation-state. On the other hand, this phenomenon also has a political expression, due to the presence of nationalist forces pursuing two objectives: the political and constitutional recognition of their differentiated identity; and political self-government in order to maintain and develop their communities as national realities. It should also be pointed out that these nationalist forces, in three cases, in addition to being strongly rooted in their respective territories, play a decisive role in the overall political system of the state (Fossas and Requejo 1999).

In these countries, the *de facto* asymmetry implied by the state's plurinational composition, as has been described, has given rise to suggesting a possible *de jure* asymmetry. That is, the establishment of constitutional differences between the units of a federation with respect to their powers and obligations, to the particular form of the central institutions, or to the application of federal laws and programmes. From the constitutional point of view, asymmetry implies the possibility of establishing a differentiated constitutional treatment for one or several territories in such a way that this avoids the principle by which all members of a federation are subject to a uniform regime, with reference to institutions and laws. De jure asymmetry, within a federal or quasi-federal system, may take various forms such as the constitutional position or nature of the units; the organisation of their internal political institutions; the structure of the sub-state legal system; the degree of political power; participation in central institutions and the reform of the constitution; or the system of finance.

On this point it is important to avoid confusing asymmetry with autonomy, a characteristic feature of all federal systems (Fossas 1995: 897). In effect, all these systems are based on the well-known idea of 'self-rule plus shared rule' which, in itself, generates diversity as it implies, for the territorial entities involved, the possibility of adopting different decisions throughout the distinct areas of the territory. From a structural point of view, it is evident that a system will be potentially characterised by far more diversity if the greater part of its affairs are decided by territorial entities, given that these units will be able to adopt different regulations and policies on many questions. In this sense, autonomy as such is the *potential* generator of diversity, and – in fact – is often confused with asymmetry. When, for example, all Canadian Provinces are granted the power to withdraw from specific constitutional reforms ('opting out'), or from given federal schemes (as is the case with the Canadian Pension Plan), then the system establishes what is only, in fact, *virtual* asymmetry, since special powers are not conceded to any of the provinces individually. Similarly, when all Spanish Autonomous Communities are granted the capacity to regulate the extent to which their respective languages may be official within their own territory, we cannot say that asymmetry, technically speaking, is in operation. Nor even when all sub-state entities are given wide-ranging powers of self-organisation. In all of these cases, the resulting heterogeneity is the consequence of the differentiated application, on the part of *some* of the entities, of powers that have been equally granted to *all other* member entities. In this way we observe that federalism has, in its own roots, a considerable capacity to reflect and accommodate whatever diversity may be manifest through factors such as religion, ethnicity, ideology, culture or nationality, and which may gain political expression. Nevertheless, in the case of the last factor, federalism does not always have the ability to provide space for complicated national realities, particularly when certain minorities feel that the diversity allowed for by autonomy simply fails to satisfy their political demands. In these cases, what such communities are really requesting is asymmetry, that is, a *special status* within the federation.

Establishing asymmetric constitutional mechanisms frequently raises questions of a technical-legal nature when it comes to applying these mechanisms to specific situations. Certain federations have resolved these difficulties with a fair degree of success by using strong doses of constitutional imagination. From this point of view, the equality between federated units, unlike that which is established between individuals, is not a necessary and immutable presupposition within a liberal democracy; rather, it is an organisational option that given constituent members may take. In addition, the establishment of this equality depends on the particular history of the federalisation process within the state in question (Pertnhaler 1998: 19).

But, as always, behind the constitutional problems there lie the political ones. The debate on asymmetry basically raises some of the great questions of conceptual and practical revision of liberal democracies at the conclusion of the twentieth century. These questions directly affect the structures and legitimisation of federalism, particularly in nationally plural societies. In effect, as I have already mentioned, federalism aims at countering the phenomenon of the nation-state by establishing a new criterion of social and political organisation. This 'new' organisation is intended to guarantee peaceful coexistence by means of articulating the plurality within a common political unit that is capable of integrating the diversity of its constituent parts.

But in spite of the fact that the federal unit is a means for composing diversity, reality demonstrates that it is not always a sufficiently flexible framework in which to accommodate, within the same political space, the nations or nationalities that currently live together in certain Western democratic societies. This is the case in the so-called 'differential societies' (Herrero de Miñón 1995: 13), that is, those in which there are communities of a national character alongside others which do not have this character, as is the case in Canada, Belgium and Spain. The constitutional experience of the last few years has taught us that there are notable difficulties in these countries when it comes to establishing a stable federal or quasi-federal structure. Several explanations have been suggested for these difficulties.

Elazar recognises that federalism has not shown itself to be an instrument that is especially well disposed towards integrating diverse nationalities into a single or general political system, unless this is accompanied by other factors tending to facilitate their integration (1987: 215). It has been said, in fact in Germany it is a widely held belief, that federalism is actually incompatible with nationalism, and wherever there are distinct nationalities, it cannot hope to prosper (Rubio Llorente 1996: 360). It has also been emphasised that nationalism is an ideology that is difficult to integrate into a federal project, since this latter not only is based upon a legal formula but also aspires to be faithful to a common project (Recalde 1995: 81). And it has been stated that it is not possible to find a constitutional formula that would be able to satisfy a nation searching for an ambiguous position, partly on the inside, partly on the outside of the State (Keating 1996: 8).

In my opinion, the development of federal or similar structures in multinational societies generates a counterposition between two points of view that are often incompatible. On the one hand there is the view of the national minority who demand political and constitutional recognition of their differentiated identity, and self-government sufficient to maintain the group as a people. And on the other hand, there is the view of the national majority who see federalism as a democratically strengthening element, and a technique by which to decentralise power in order to heighten the efficiency of the management of public affairs. Evidence for the tension between these two points of view can be seen clearly in the three countries mentioned above: in Belgium there is the divergence of political inclinations between the Flemings (cultural 'communitarisation') and the Walloons (economical regionalisation); in Canada there is the contrast between the demands for greater autonomy on the part of Quebec, and the need to reinforce the federal government expressed by the other Provinces; and in Spain there are the differences between the projects set out by the Basque and Catalan nationalists, and those of the state-wide political parties (the conservative Partido Popular (PP) and the socialist Partido Socialista Obrero Español (PSOE)). In situations such as these, the generalisation and equalisation of autonomy is brought about in agreement with the majority view: it is difficult to make this process compatible with the views held by the minority.

In reality, the counterposition between these ways of understanding the situation arises from the connection between asymmetry and plurinationality, present in the debate that is taking place in these three countries. The terms and the positions that are maintained clearly indicate the important role played by political identity in this discussion. That is, what is of great significance in the eyes of the citizens concerned is the way in which they perceive their 'belonging' to a particular community over which political institutions are then constructed. Differences in this perception are traditionally related to the positions adopted in the discussions over asymmetry. The differences between the degree to which self-government is wished for correspond to justifications which are likewise very diverse. And this, in turn, results in disparate conceptions of equality between 'national' and 'regional' territorial units. For the *national* units, guaranteeing the regions the same powers as those granted to the nations implies a negating of the minority's equality, reducing its status to a regional division within the national majority. In contrast, the *regional* units see the concession of special powers to the minorities as a recognition that certain territorial units are less important than others and, in consequence, it views these concessions as discriminatory to the citizens as a whole. In fact, the demand for a *special status* on the part of the national minorities is directed not only towards an increase in powers but also towards their recognition as a nation (Kymlicka 1998: 27). And these positions reflect deeper differences over the very concept of federation: for the minorities, federalism is, above all, an association between founding peoples on an equal footing, an association which demands asymmetry between national and regional territorial units; for the majorities, however, federalism is basically a union between equal territorial units, and this notion, in contrast to that of the minority, demands symmetry.[1] On the other hand, national minorities often conceive of the structure of the state more as a confederation than as a federation. Their basic demand does not consist of defending the view that the political community is culturally plural, but rather it sustains the idea that there is more than one political community, each of which has the right to self-government.

Demands on the part of minority nationalism for asymmetry – understood as a desire for 'autonomy-differentiation' that brings with it a *special status* for one or several communities – has normally resulted in strong opposition in all countries. Shared experience also shows that the pressure applied by minority nationalism in favour of achieving asymmetry is usually responded to with pressure applied in favour of symmetry on the part of state nationalism. The arguments used by this second group differ according to country, but there is a notable similarity between the basic positions. It is clear, in this sense, that state nationalism tends to use a belligerent rhetoric with communities that proclaim themselves to be national. This rhetoric consistently negates the national character of the minority community, tries to delegitimise the discourse of nationalist parties, and aims at drawing an end to the decisive position that the minority community might have in the governability of the State (Bastida 1998: 195). This represents, in effect, a political fight between 'nationalisms', between forces that give support to different *nation-building* projects, and an important part of this conflict takes place on symbolic ground, a territory which thereby gains considerable importance. For this reason, demands for the recognition of plurinationality run from constitutional language to the use of anthems and flags, to questions of protocol, to international 'presence' or to the use of diverse languages in official documents, on currency and within the institutions of the various communities (Requejo 1999). In this area, state nationalism tends to project a uni-national image of the state, and resists any symbology that may express its compound nature.

Another argument against asymmetry has been the representation in central institutions of communities with a special status. Detractors of asymmetric federalism maintain that if such a system were to exist, communities with greater powers ought to have less weight within federal institutions and, in any case, their representatives ought not to have the power to decide affairs at a federal level that their community could decide at a territorial level, since this would then place them in a privileged situation. The issue was already under discussion in the nineteenth century in the United Kingdom in reference to Home Rule for Ireland, and the so-called 'West Lothian Question' has emerged again in the new devolution process for Scotland and Wales that was initiated in 1998. In Canada (Dion 1994: 180) and Spain, the subject has also been raised in similar terms. It is a question of great complexity from the theoretical point of view (Keating 1998: 106; Kymlicka 1996: 40), and is undoubtedly an issue for which a political resolution is particularly difficult.

As I have already observed, another important argument used to oppose asymmetry is that such a situation would imply the concession of unfounded privileges for determined units, and this would go against the notion of equality among all the federated parts. This principle, although not normally written into the Constitution, is nevertheless considered to be politically valid within the system. And it is from this position that the demands made by national units are rejected by other units, or, as in the case of Spain, that the demands are only generally acceptable if they become applicable to one and all, a fact that often provokes yet more resistance on the part of central government.

Beyond any doubt, however, one of the arguments that generates the greatest opposition to asymmetry is that which considers it unacceptable since it undermines equality between the citizens of the country, and their rights and obligations. The asymmetric distribution of powers between entities, or the asymmetric representation of territorial units in federal institutions, would lead to inequality between the citizens of different communities. And this would go against the long sought-after universal character of civil, political and social rights. This question – equality between citizens within a federal system, and particularly a multinational federal system – leads me to the final part of my argument.

## Multinational federalism and equality among citizens

As I have indicated, federalism emerged in order to provide an answer to diverse phenomena within modern political life. This included reacting to the decline of the old aristocratic foundations in the premodern era by opting in favour of new principles based on equality, and giving rise to the appearance of the modern nation-state. In fact, these two phenomena developed in parallel. The nation-state, in any of its forms, has tended towards the concentration of power, whereas the rise of equality has tended towards the homogenisation of the relations between the power and the population, by means of attributing common citizenship to all individuals resident in a territory. The principle of equality before the law, formulated in the French and North American revolutions, expresses this idea with absolute clarity.

Nevertheless, there is a certain tension between equality of citizens and the federal principle. Contrary to a unitary state, federal structures allow the entities that are integrated within the federation to formulate their own rules and policies in their jurisdiction, leaving other matters in the hand of the central government. This results in a diversity of legal systems that are in conflict with the strict equality among the citizens (Woehrling 1991: 122). In other words, 'federalism and rights are necessarily at odds, for federalism countenances particularism and encourages diversity, while the protection of rights seems to require universal standards and uniform treatment' (Katz and Tarr 1996: x). Perhaps it was for this reason that Tocqueville said that the modern road to individual equality could well be a foreboding of the death of federalism, since only a centralised government can guarantee equality in any depth. What is true, however, is that there are no unitary states which have achieved 'equality in depth'; and those states which, from the time of the French revolution, have claimed to do so have instead produced inequality and – all too often – tyranny.

If we focus on legal equality, it is evident that if this implies all citizens having to live according to the same laws, this is – as a consequence – radically opposed to federalism. Federalism, in contrast, implies that equality has to be reconciled to the existence of different laws being applicable to different territorial communities. As the Supreme Court has stated in Canada, the distribution of powers not only allows for differentiated treatment according to the Province of residence, but also authorises and encourages distinctions of a geographical kind. There can be no doubt that unequal treatment resulting from the exercising of these responsibilities by provincial legislators should not be attacked for the fact of creating distinctions founded on the Province of residence (R.C. Sheldon, [1990] 2 R.C.S.254).

As for political equality, federal systems have gradually been introducing equality in voting, and the US Supreme Court has reinforced the idea through its jurisprudence (*Baker v. Carr, 1962; Reynolds v. Sims, 1964*). However, this principle has been demanded internally for the states, but not in relation to the Federation, where there is an unequal representation in Congress, in the Senate and in the Presidential elections. Curiously, on one occasion when the State of Maryland called on the federal Senate to organise its upper chamber, the Supreme Court declared that 'this organisation was historically the product of a compromise to avoid the threat of seeing the abortion of the birth of our nation' (*Maryland v. Tawes, 1964*).

Finally, social and economic equality require the burdens and benefits produced by the government to be distributed in as fair a way as possible between individuals and communities. However, the existence of territorial political entities with the powers of financial collection and spending mean that the distribution of a part of the benefits is unequal throughout the territory, even if within the state in general this distribution is broadly equal. We could argue that these inequalities are not questionable if they have been decided democratically, that is, if the citizens in a given state have all had the same chance to decide, by themselves, if they choose to be more or less equal than others. However, the fact that there are inequalities that are the result of undesirable causes could well justify the redistributive intervention of the federal government through a number of different ways.

These three aspects of equality in a federal state allow us to claim that a system of this type makes it possible for citizens to choose between those rights, responsibilities and benefits that they consider to be fundamental, and which should therefore correspond to all citizens, and those which may vary according to citizen preference in different territorial units. What is true, however, is that the social and political evolution in the nineteenth century has given rise to the predomination of a political culture of the universalisation of rights that tends towards a homogenisation of citizen status within the state as a whole, in spite of the fact that this may have a federal structure. This tendency has occurred in the majority of modern federal states, and has been made specific in the adoption of charters of rights, applicable to all citizens independently of territory, which are interpreted in the final instance by a single judicial authority called the Supreme Court, or the Constitutional Tribunal. It is evident that this has led to the progressive reduction of the disparity that existed in the original federal systems, and has produced a tendency towards uniformity, though not always towards centralisation.

In the case of the United States, the Bill of Rights added to the federal Constitution in 1791 was originally applied only to the federal government, as the Supreme Court had occasion to recognise (*Barron v. Baltimore, 1833*). The subsequent approval of the Fourteenth Amendment that was given after the Civil War (1868) was used until the beginning of the twentieth century, basically as a means of protecting property rights against the actions of the states. But, from 1937, the affair of Roosevelt's 'Court-Packing Plan' brought about the abandonment on the part of the Supreme Court of its obstructionist attitude towards the measures of the New Deal, and the Fourteenth Amendment began to have repercussions for civil liberties. In fact, in the heart of the Supreme Court itself there was a debate on the doctrine of substantive 'due process', which for some judges meant that the Fourteenth Amendment aimed at 'nationalising' the Charter of Rights and Liberties (Katz 1991: 42). The arrival of Judge Warren to the Presidency of the US Supreme Court set in motion a revolution in the area of rights and liberties that was also to affect the federal structure. Specifically, it put into action the definitive nationalisation of the Charter, now applicable to all states, and the understanding that the rights were an aspect of citizenship. This created a kind of standard for rights, below which no state could descend. The Supreme Court has subsequently lowered this level, and the Supreme Courts of the states, in interpreting their own constitutions, have been able to establish higher standards giving rise to a phenomenon known as the New Judicial Federalism (Kincaid 1988: 163), and which produces greater diversity with respect to the protection of rights.

In the case of Canada, the British North American Act did not contain a Charter of Rights, and such a charter was not to be incorporated until the 'repatriation' of the Constitution in 1982, not entering into effect until 1985. The charter guarantees the citizens' right to equality (art. 15), but at the same time it retains some of the dispositions from the 1867 Constitution which protect the rights of certain groups defined in terms of their language or religion (arts. 93 and 13), and it incorporates other dispositions which protect the indigenous peoples and the multicultural patrimony of the Canadians (art. 27). In addition, it includes a curious 'notwithstanding' clause (art. 33) which allows the legislature of a Province to pass a law declaring that a given provincial provision is valid in spite of being in contradiction to some of the Charter's dispositions.

Despite the initial fears that certain Provinces had concerning the Charter's homogenising effects and the repercussions that this might have on provincial powers, its application and interpretation on the part of the Supreme Court has not had the unifying or centralising effects that were expected (Woehrling 1991: 168), as the famous Ford case illustrates (*Ford v. P.G. Québec,* [1998] 2 R.C.S.712). This, and the already mentioned New Judicial Federalism, demonstrate that the evolution of the political culture of equality and the universality of rights has had a clear effect on federal systems, but these are still able to tolerate levels of diversity that are simply not possible in the unitary states.

At this point we need to remind ourselves about the distinction between multinational federations and territorial federations. The examples of the USA and Canada show that, in spite of federalism's capacity to protect diversity in the area of rights, this becomes rather more difficult in multinational societies where the political culture of the minority nations may well not coincide fully with that of the majority nationals. Precisely because the issue of rights is so closely linked to the political culture, the cultural composition of states acquires great relevance, as does the existence of majorities and minorities that may or may not coincide at a federal and territorial level. Universalist arguments do not allow for variations in the rights of a multinational state because they defend the recognition of universal rights and values and, therefore, also oppose any asymmetric solution on this point. In reality, what claims to be universalism often hides the predominance of a determined political culture, that of the majority, which is also based on particularist values. And it is often the case, in addition, that a single Charter of Rights in a federal state, as the US and Canadian cases illustrate, has the clear intention of nation-building on the part of the majority. It is obvious that the framework of rights established by law always incorporates characteristics of a particular society and of its culture. On the other hand, the process of interpreting rights implies the adoption of specific cultural values that assume given notions of what is meant by a 'nation' and a 'culture'. That is, a multinational society may well require the regulation and interpretation of rights that bear in mind cultural differences.

We have now come to the final part of this discussion concerning citizen equality in multinational states that adopt asymmetric federal forms. As we have observed, one of the main arguments for rejecting asymmetry is that it may lead to inequality among citizens, given that those who belong to communities with a special status will reap the benefit of greater powers and rights than those available to other territorial entities. Yet this argument is not acceptable, because asymmetry does not refer so much to citizens in possession of *more* power as to *where* that power is exercised. Asymmetry means that the exercising of power with respect to given territorial entities is divided in a different way, so that certain questions that are decided at a central level by the majority citizens are decided at a regional level by minority citizens. The change of division between central and territorial power therefore responds to variations in the perception of political identity, present in multinational societies, and this is its justification (Webber 1994: 230). It is a justification which, in my opinion, allows the necessary adaptation of the principles of federal democracy, and specifically that of equality, to the demands of cultural pluralism at the end of the twentieth century.

## Conclusions

In this chapter I have touched on various aspects of equality in federal states, especially those of a plurinational nature. As for equality between founding peoples, we have observed that, in certain historical examples, this has not been fully achieved since the diversity between the founding entities has led to the belief (held by some of these entities) that certain groups should have a special position within the constitutional pact. On the other hand, processes of federation have often been processes of nation-building, which have given rise to political unions whose character has later been argued over, as is the case with the USA or Canada.

The modern nation-state has brought about the progressive tendency to unify the plurality of premodern political structures, and to implant a political culture based on the democratic equality of its citizens. Federalism has tried to respond to this phenomenon by maintaining a 'pactist' notion of power, and by inventing an organisation that keeps it divided, thereby allowing for the integration of territorial plurality within a constitutional unit. In spite of the tendency towards homogenisation in the majority of modern federal systems, federalism still allows for certain diversity, whereas this is not the case with unitary states. Nevertheless, the development of federal structures in multinational states is particularly difficult and continues to come into conflict, in a number of ways, with the concept of equality that has accompanied the nation-state.

The search for cultural recognition at the close of the twentieth century, and most specifically, the demands made by minority nationalism has once more brought to the fore the question of equality for the integrating units of a federal state. In the West, Canada, Belgium and Spain provide the example of three countries in which there has been considerable debate on federal asymmetry linked to the plurinational character of the state. This becomes an issue when certain federated entities demand to be recognised as 'national' communities, while others identify themselves as regions of the majority nation. And there is a clear political expression of these views with the presence of nationalist forces, rooted within these communities, making a plea for the recognition of their differentiated identity, and for a special constitutional status within the federation. The difficulty of establishing stable federal forms in such contexts is due to the contrasting ways of viewing the situation that exist within each group's political identity. And this leads to different understandings of equality among territorial entities and to profound discrepancies over the nature of the federation itself. For this reason, demands for asymmetry have met with strong opposition in these three countries.

One of the main arguments against asymmetry has been that it contradicts the principle of equality among all citizens. The argument maintains that every individual should have the benefit of the same rights, of a universal character. In fact, this principle conflicts with the federal principle that allows different territorial entities to formulate their own regulations and policies within their particular fields of competence, from which we derive a wide range of legal systems throughout a given territory.

In spite of the progressive implantation of a culture of equality in modern federal systems, expressed in the acceptance of Charters of rights interpreted in the final instance by a single judicial authority, federal systems have shown themselves to be more tolerant of legal diversity than unitary states have, and have thereby made it possible to balance their citizens' wishes to be simultaneously different and equal.

This balance is more difficult to achieve in plurinational societies, where differences in political culture may bring about differences in values and rights between the diverse communities. This might require a regulation and interpretation of rights that bear in mind these cultural differences. In reality, the framework of rights established by the law always incorporates characteristics of a particular society, and of its culture. On the other hand, the process of interpreting rights implies the adoption of certain given social values that, in themselves, have a determined notion of what 'nation' and 'culture' mean.

Proposals for asymmetry in this ambit have provoked opposition since it is thought that, by granting a special status to a community, the citizens of that group will have greater power and rights than those of other groups. Nevertheless, asymmetry simply means that the exercise of power with respect to certain entities is divided in different ways, and that certain questions decided at a central level by the citizens of the majority are decided at a regional level by the citizens of the minority. The alteration of the division between central and regional power therefore responds to variations in the perception of political identity, democratically expressed in a pluricultural society.

In short, the accommodation of complex cultural realities, among which there are plurinational societies, demands the revision of the postulates of the nation-state, of the principles of federalism, and of the very idea of equality itself.

# Acknowledgements

This work forms part of the research project 'Federalismo, igualdad y diferencia' (Federalism, equality and difference) (DGICYT PB96–0972) funded by the Spanish Ministry of Education and Culture, 1998, through the 'Programa sectorial de Promoción del Conocimiento'.

# Note

1 This contrast of notions is well illustrated in the political debate in Canada where, historically, two visions of federalism have faced off against each other: that of provincial autonomy *versus* that of provincial equality, as is clearly explained in Vipond 1995.

# References

Bastida, X. (1998), *La Nación española y el nacionalismo constitucional*, Madrid, Ariel.

Beer, S.H. (1994), *To Make a Nation: The Rediscovery of American Federalism*, Cambridge, Mass., Harvard University Press.

Cairns, A.C. (1991), 'Constitutional Change and the Three Equalities', in R.L.Watts and D.M. Brown (eds) *Options for a New Canada*, Toronto, University of Toronto Press.

Dion, S. (1994), 'Le fédéralisme fortement asymétrique: improbable et indésirable', in F. Leslie Seide (ed.) *Seeking a New Canadian Partnership: Asymmetrical and Confederal Options*, Montreal, Institute for Research on Public Policy.

Elazar, D. (1987), *Exploring Federalism*, Tuscaloosa, Al., University of Alabama Press.

Fossas, E. (1995), 'Asimetría y autonomía', *Informe Pi i Sunyer sobre Comunidades Autónomas 1994*, Barcelona, Fundació Carles Pi i Sunyer d'Estudis Autonòmics i Locals.

Fossas, E. and Requejo, F. (1999), *Asimetría federal y Estado plurinacional: El debate sobre la acomodación de la diversidad en Canadá, Bélgica y España*, Madrid, Trotta.

García Pelayo, M. (1984), *Derecho Constitucional comparado*, Madrid, Alianza Universidad.

Guibernau, M. (1996), *Los nacionalismos*, Barcelona, Ariel.

Herrero de Miñón, M. (1995), 'La posible diversidad de los modelos autonómicos en la transición, en la Constitución española de 1978 y en los Estatutos de Autonomía', AA.DD., *Uniformidad y diversidad de las Comunidades Autónomas*, Barcelona, Institut d'Estudis Autonòmics.

Katz, E. (1991), 'Les Etats Unis', in Edmond Orban *et al.*, *Fédéralisme et Cours Suprêmes / Federalism and Supreme Courts*, Brussels and Montreal, Bruylant–Les Presses de l'Université de Montréal.

Katz, E. and Tarr, G.A. (eds) (1996), *Federalism and Rights*, Boston, Mass., Rowman & Littlefield.

Keating, M. (1996), *Naciones contra el Estado: El nacionalismo de Cataluña, Quebec y Escocia*, Barcelona, Ariel.

Keating, M. (1998), 'Principes et problèmes du gouvernement asymétrique', *Politique et Sociétés*, 17, 3.

Kincaid, J. (1988), 'State Court Protections of Individual Rights under State Constitutions: The New Judicial Federalism', *Journal of State Government*, 61.

Kincaid, J. (1991), 'Federalism', in Ch.F. Bahmueller (ed.) *Civitas: A Framework for Civic Education*, Calabasas, Center for Civic Education.

Kymlicka, W. (1996), 'Federalismo, nacionalismo y multiculturalismo', *Revista Internacional de Filosofía Política*, 7.

Kymlicka, W. (1998), 'Le fédéralisme multinational au Canada: un partenariat à repenser', in Guy Laforest and Roger Gibbins (eds) *Sortir de l'impasse. Les voies de la réconciliation*, Montreal, Institute for Research on Public Policy.

Laband, P. (1900), *Le Droit Public de l'Empire Allemand*, vol. 1, Paris.

Lenaerts, K. (1990), 'Constitutionalism and the Many Faces of Federalism', *American Journal of Comparative Law*, 38.

Madison, J. (1908), *Journal of the Debates in the Convention which framed the Constitution*, vol. 2, New York, G.P. Putnam's Sons.

Pernthaler, P. (1998), *Lo stato federale differenziato*, Bologna, Il Mulino.

Recalde, J.R. (1995), *Crisis y descomposición de la política*, Madrid, Alianza Universidad.

Requejo, F. (1999), 'Pluralism, Nationalism and Federalism: A Revision of Democratic Citizenship in Plurinational States', *European Journal of Political Research*, 35, 2.

Resnick, Ph. (1994), 'Towards a Multinational Federalism: Asymmetrical and Confederal Alternatives', in F. Leslie Seidle (ed.) *Seeking a New Canadian Partnership: Asymmetrical and Confederal Options*, Montreal, Institute for Research on Public Policy.

Rocher, F. and Smith, M. (1995), 'Four Dimensions of the Canadian Constitutional Debate', in F. Rocher and M. Smith, *New Trends in Canadian Federalism*, Ontario, Broadview Press.

Rubio Llorente, F. (1993), *La forma del poder (Estudios sobre la Constitución)*, Madrid, Centro de Estudios Constitucionales.

Rubio Llorente, F. (1996), 'La reforma constitucional del Senado', AA.DD., *Ante el futuro del Senado*, Barcelona, Institut d'Estudis Autonòmics.

Sartori, G. (1992), *Elementos de teoría política*, Madrid, Alianza Universidad.

Tarlton, Ch.D. (1965), 'Symmetry and Asymmetry as Elements of Federalism: A Theoretical Speculation', *Journal of Politics*, 27.

Tully, J. (1995), *Strange Multiplicity: Constitutionalism in an Age of Diversity*, Cambridge, Cambridge University Press.

Vipond, R. (1995), 'From Provincial Autonomy to Provincial Equality (Or, Clyde Wells and the Distinct Society)', in J.H. Carens (ed.) *Is Quebec Nationalism Just? Perspectives from Anglophone Canada*, Montreal, McGill-Queens University Press.

Watts, R.L. (1994), 'Contemporary Views on Federalism', in B. De Villiers (ed.) *Evaluating Federal Systems*, Cape Town, South Africa, Juta.

Webber, J. (1994), *Reimagining Canada: Language, Culture, Community and the Canadian Constitution*, Montreal, McGill-Queen's University Press.

Woehrling, J. (1991), 'Le principe d'égalité, la système fédéral canadien et le caractère distinct du Québec', in Pierre Patenaude (dir.), *Québec-Communauté française de Belgique: Autonomie et spécificité dans le cadre d'un système fédéral*, Montreal, Wilson & Lafleur.

# 5　Secession and (constitutional) democracy

## Wayne Norman

### Introduction

Is secession democratic? Would an adequate theory of democracy include a right for groups of people to choose to secede from their state, taking a portion of its territory with them? The moral evaluation of secession is now a small boom industry in political philosophy, and many theorists are convinced that the answer to these questions is obviously Yes. Secession, they argue, is the ultimate act of self-determination, and self-determination in turn is the core idea of democracy. If democratic citizens can be entrusted to decide how they should be governed, who should govern them, and what the government should do, why then should they not also be allowed to decide the frontiers of the state in which their self-government should take place?[1]

Other theorists are quick to point out numerous points of tension between the ideas of democracy and secession.[2] The possibility of secession could actually undermine democracy, they warn. The integrity of majority rule is subverted when a group threatens not to abide by democratic decisions, but rather to secede, if it happens to find itself in the minority (Buchanan 1991, pp. 98–99; 1998, p. 21). In a similar way, they argue, the spectre of secession undermines the deliberative aspect of democracy. Democracy is not just a matter of weighing preferences fairly; it is also a forum of deliberation, where participants develop and modify their views after discussion. If exit is too easy an option, however, this kind of deliberation will not take place (Buchanan 1991, p. 134; 1998, p. 22). Third, these theorists sometimes highlight a paradox in the idea that it is natural for democratic deliberations to be extended from matters of government and policy to matters of choosing a polity. In effect, democracy is rule by the people; but this assumes we already know who the people are, who the 'self' is that is self-determining. Yet this is exactly what secession calls into question.

A vote on secession is, in large part, a vote to decide who will be the people forming the self-governing polity. But can this matter be decided by a vote? Who would get to vote? We would already need an answer to the question 'who are the people?' in order to know who could vote; and yet this is what the vote is to decide.[3]

A fourth problem with too straightforward a link between democratic ideals and a right to secession underlies all three of these worries. It is misleading to equate democracy with simple majority rule, or to assume that majority rule necessarily trumps other fundamental values and rights in a liberal democracy.[4] An act of secession, or even an attempted secession, can have a profound impact on the rights and legitimate expectations of citizens both within and outside of the seceding region. It can change people's citizenship against their will. It can create new minority groups whose members may have good reason to fear the worst. It can fundamentally change the nature of the original state without the citizens living in the rump having ever had a direct say in the matter. It can create uncertainties in financial markets along with new trade barriers that leave both the new state and the rump state worse off. And, of course, in many parts of the world, it raises the spectre of ongoing violence (as in the Punjab and Northern Ireland) and brutal methods of forced expulsion (as in the Balkans).

These reasons suggest that whatever the link between democracy and the right of secession, it will not be a simple deductive inference from abstract concepts of self-determination and majority rule. This is not to deny that there are certainly cases where secession is legitimate, and where it is both appropriate and indeed imperative that it be legitimated by democratic processes. In order to determine more clearly when secession is justified, and what specific democratic procedures should apply, I propose that we inquire about how secessionist politics should be regulated within the constitutional framework of a modern democratic state.

We can say in a meaningful way that secession follows from, or is compatible with, democracy if we can specify a reasonable procedure for secession within a just, democratic constitutional order. In this chapter, as a first step in such an inquiry, I shall ask a simple question: *is it appropriate for there to be a secession clause in the constitution of a democratic state?* I shall not be discussing at length here the issue of what such a clause should look like,[5] although to make the question interesting we have to assume that a fair secession clause – one compatible with norms of democratic legitimacy – would allow certain kinds of territorially defined groups (e.g., provinces in a federation) to secede if this is what the clear majority in the group clearly wants to do.

## Constitutionalising secession: probing the case against

Although there is a burgeoning literature on the right to secession, much less attention has been paid to the issue of whether or how this right might be constitutionalised in the domestic law of a democratic state. Perhaps the most extensive discussion of this topic has come from an opponent of constitutionalising secession, Cass Sunstein. In a way, Sunstein is articulating and defending the orthodoxy since, after all, no more than a handful of states actually recognise a right to secession within their constitutions. In a ground-breaking yet rarely cited article from 1991, Cass Sunstein summarises concisely most of the reasons for thinking that democratic constitutions should *not* include a secession clause (despite the fact that he thinks secession is sometimes morally justified).

> To place such a right in a founding document would increase the risks of ethnic and factional struggle; reduce the prospects for compromise and deliberation in government; raise dramatically the stakes of day-to-day political decisions; introduce irrelevant and illegitimate considerations into those decisions; create dangers of blackmail, strategic behaviour, and exploitation; and most generally, endanger the prospects for long-term self-governance.
>
> (Sunstein 1991, p. 634)

Sunstein's reason for keeping a right of secession out of the constitution follows from his view of constitutions as, among other things, a set of precommitment strategies. The idea is that the sorts of distortions to democratic decision-making which he believes a secession clause would engender are exactly what wise founding parties should be trying to avoid; and they do this by 'precommitting' themselves to a constitutional regime that discourages such distortions.

> If the right to secede exists, each subunit will be vulnerable to threats of secession by the others. If the considerations marshalled thus far are persuasive, all or most subunits are quite plausibly better off if each of them waives its right to secede. More generally, the difficulty or impossibility of exit from the nation will encourage cooperation for the long term.
>
> (Sunstein 1991, p. 650)

So, for Sunstein, they would not rationally agree to constitutionalise secession; and this is tantamount to arguing that a right to secession ought not to be recognised in the constitution.

I think Sunstein is entirely correct in highlighting the distortions of secessionist *politics* in a democratic state. All of the effects he mentioned do in fact appear in some form in multination democracies – such as Canada, Belgium, the United Kingdom and Spain – with nationalist-secessionist movements. The crucial question for the issue at hand, however, is whether secessionist politics would be more likely to be *fuelled* or *choked* by 'legalising' secession. This is a question for political psychology and sociology, and it is far from clear that Sunstein's pessimism is justified.

He has no doubt uncovered a genuine causal mechanism whereby a constitutional secession clause could encourage the leaders of subunits (or whichever kinds of groups are explicitly given access to the right to secede) to make more credible threats to secede if they do not get the concessions they want on a wide range of political issues.[6] Let us call this a 'fuelling mechanism', since it fuels secessionist politics. It is not, of course, the only fuelling mechanism. It is obvious, for example, that oppression and exploitation of a region can also fuel secessionist politics. And even in the absence of injustice, so can the presence of minority-group nationalism, complete with the currency of the views that the minority group in question constitutes a nation, and that nations have an inherent right to self-determination and ultimately to secession if they choose it.

There must also be a number of what we might call 'choking mechanisms' for secessionist politics, since only a very small percentage of the potential national minorities (where potentiality is found in ethnic and linguistic distinctiveness) ever produce full-blown national identities, let alone secessionist movements. Brutal repression of minority-nationalist leaders is one (literally) obvious choking mechanism, but this is not an option in a democratic state. Guarantees of minority rights, including those institutionalised in a federal system, is another choking mechanism in many states (although it could be argued that this also sets up a possible fuelling mechanism by allowing minorities political structures with which to build their distinct political identities).

The interesting question for the problem at hand, however, is whether, *pace* Sunstein, a constitutional clause for secession could also serve as a *choking* mechanism for secessionist politics in some states. Consider the case of a multination state whose founders agreed at its point of inception to include what Sunstein describes as a qualified right to secede. Let us suppose that the main qualification on the right is that a two-thirds majority within the region must agree to secede on a referendum with a clear question.[7] Since the state was founded (or refounded, say, in the case of a state liberated from an empire) with enthusiasm from all parties to continue, we can imagine that such a clause may stay on the books, so to speak, for years or generations without there ever being a serious secessionist challenge. (Keep in mind the distinct lack of 'secession' threats in the European Union, despite fundamental opposition by some member states to certain policies and the fact that unilateral withdrawal is possible without even having to hold a referendum.) The longer such a secession clause remains, the more legitimate it becomes; in particular, the more legitimate the requirement for a supermajority. (Few serious political actors in the USA, e.g., question the legitimacy of the various qualified majorities required in American politics for, among other things, constitutional amendments, the removal of a sitting President, or congressional override of a President's veto.)

Now how might the existence of such a clause serve as a choking mechanism for secession? Primarily by being more demanding than the implicit 'democratic' threshold of a simple majority which secessionist leaders would insist upon in the absence of a formal constitutional provision. If the 'natural' level of support for secession in a particular region is somewhat less than 50 per cent (as it is, e.g., in Quebec, Scotland, Flanders, Catalonia, the Spanish Basque Country, Corsica and Northern Italy, to name just some of the likely candidates for secession from democratic states), nationalist leaders may nevertheless be encouraged by the possibility of raising support above that threshold through a concerted campaign of nationalist politics. They may do this in order to reinforce demands and threats within the system, or because they actually do prefer secession. But if it is clear that a supermajority is required, they might consider it futile to try to construct the sort of nationalist sentiments and grievances necessary to convince such a strong majority within an otherwise reasonably just democratic system to vote for the uncertainties of secession. Such a clause then would clearly be serving as a choking mechanism not only for secession but also for secessionist politics and minority-nationalist politics more generally.

Of course it is easy to identify mechanisms of political psychology; the real problem for social science is to predict which ones are likely to be activated in any given situation. Would a secession clause serve as a fuelling mechanism, as Sunstein insists, by giving rise to credible secessionist threats where they would not otherwise have occurred; or is it the case that secessionist threats will often occur, as they do in our world, even in the absence of a secession clause, and that they might in fact be 'choked' by a legitimate clause requiring a supermajority (or some other form of 'constitutional hurdle')?

It seems to me pretty obvious that the answer to this question will vary from state to state. In some political cultures that do not otherwise experience secessionist pressures, including perhaps the United States, a secession clause might serve as a fuelling mechanism. In others, it might well choke potential secessionist movements by placing the threshold of necessary support high enough to render secessionist threats non-credible and secessionist mobilisations counterproductive. This suggests, at the very least, that Sunstein's rather sweeping conclusion against the advisability of constitutional recognition of a right to secede is unjustified. This is true even of the more specific case of newly liberated Eastern Europe states, which were the object of Sunstein's reflections. At the time he wrote the article, these included the former Warsaw Pact states, Yugoslavia and Albania, and the still-constituted Soviet Union along with its possible successor states. This group includes such a vast range of political cultures, historical circumstances, ethnic and territorial divisions, that it would be very difficult to assume almost *any* empirical generalisations holding for politics in these regions.

## Constitutionalising secession: further reasons in favour

In addition to the possibility of a secession clause serving as a choking rather than a fuelling mechanism for secessionist politics, there are several other reasons for thinking that such a clause would be appropriate, or at least not inappropriate, in the constitutions of some democratic multination states.

It could be argued that most constitutional democracies already have secession clauses built into their constitutional amending formulas, but that in such a form these clauses are manifestly unfair. A normal constitutional amending procedure could always be used to write a sub-unit out of the constitution, so to speak, by changing the international frontiers of the state to exclude the territory in question. This procedure would not always be fair to secessionist regions, however, because a typical amending formula gives veto powers to the central government, and in federations to the other subunits. Hence, if a subunit wanted to secede because it found itself exploited or systematically outvoted in majoritarian decision-making – a condition that most theorists believe justifies secession – it would have to rely on the support of the very groups and institutions that had flouted its interests up to that point.

A just secession clause would, presumably, make the will of the people in the subunit (or territory defined in some other way) a decisive condition for secession, or at least for the legitimacy of negotiations leading to secession.

Similarly, secession could be seen as the logical extreme of other legitimate constitutional features, such as a federal division of powers or the power of legislative nullification. Secession is similar to a subunit exercising a right of nullification on every piece of federal legislation and enacting its own in place; or more directly, it is like granting a subunit all or virtually all of powers that are normally split between the federal and subunit governments in a federation. All federal constitutions allow for changes in the division of powers. So again, it could be argued, a secession clause would not be a wholly unusual instrument in a modern constitution; it is just the logical extreme of features that already exist.

The existence of a secession clause that is not used can come to be seen as evidence that the state is united by consent and not force. This could be a powerful symbol in the political culture. It would be considerably more difficult for secessionists to develop myths of historical oppression or grievance if the minority group in question had always had a right to secede which it had never sought to exploit.

Finally, we can argue that where popular secessionist politics do arise, the situation is crying out for some sort of legal framework for the fair and orderly resolution of this kind of political contest. A democratic secessionist debate will be carried out much as other processes in democratic politics are, complete with referendum campaigns conducted under fair legislation, and with Yes- and No-sides led by the major political parties. And yet, in the event of a victory for the secessionists, we would see that this whole process remains outside of constitutional norms. Secessionists are likely to insist on the democratic credentials of a simple majority as sufficient to justify secession, and the central government is likely (with reason) to see a narrow victory in favour as insufficient. In the absence of prearranged rules for secessionist contests, a victory for secessionists in a referendum amounts to little more than the strengthening of the secessionists' hand in a game of power politics. Situations like this in many parts of the world invite cycles of violence. But even where state or paramilitary violence is unlikely, such stand-offs will be disruptive for normal political and economic life. Emotionally charged positions on both sides combined with jittery international markets make possible a mutually disadvantageous situation of the sort that both parties might want pre-arranged constitutional measures to avoid. Even if there is a large enough majority in favour of secession to make the central government realise that it cannot legitimately hold onto the territory, there are many points of negotiation that will not necessarily be resolved fairly given the relative bargaining strengths of the two sides. These issues include the problem of parts of the subunit wanting to stay with the larger state and parts of the larger state wanting to secede with the subunit; as well as questions about the division of central government properties and the splitting of debts or surpluses. A fair formula of division could be agreed to by parties founding the original union; but not necessarily by parties negotiating a secession agreement. A final reason for thinking that this process should be governed by legal procedures and not just power politics is that a legal process would ensure that there was never a break with the rule of law. This would minimise the risk of violence, but beyond that it can be thought of as an almost intrinsically worthy aim in a constitutional democracy.

The analogy with divorce is helpful in this context (see Bauböck 1999). Sunstein himself refers to the analogy, noting that

> A decision to stigmatize divorce or to make it available only under certain conditions – as virtually every state in the United States has done – may lead to happier as well as more stable marriages, by providing an incentive for spouses to adapt their behavior and even their desires to promote long-term harmony.
>
> (Sunstein 1991, p. 649)

Similarly, Sunstein argues, 'in the secession context there are strong reasons for making exit difficult' (1991, p. 650). Of course, I agree. But, the analogy seems to work directly against Sunstein's case. Why should the difficulty of secession come from the uncertainties of an unprecedented political stand-off? The great *dis*analogy between divorce and secession is that the former is within a legal framework – indeed, the idea of divorce, as opposed to mere permanent separation, just *is* a legal concept – while the latter remains outside of both international law,[8] and the domestic constitutional law of the great majority of states today.[9] Or to put it another way, international law currently gives states the right to treat their seceding regions the way husbands had a right to treat their 'disobedient' wives until well into the twentieth century.[10] There is a big difference between making divorce or secession difficult within a legal framework, on the one hand, and allowing the stronger party to decide more or less unilaterally just how difficult it is going to be, on the other. The logical conclusion from the analogy with legalised divorce is that secessionist politics should be brought within the rule of law.

## Secession and the multination state

I should emphasise at this point that nothing in my argument should be read as evidence of enthusiasm for secession. On the contrary, there is something most regrettable about secession in the context of otherwise just democratic states. Whatever the facts on the ground, such secessions stand out as symbols of intolerance. Since virtually all serious secessionist movements are based on ethnic cleavages (no matter how civic and democratic the secessionists' rhetoric and ideals) no liberal can be cheered by the admission of two or more ethnocultural groups that they are incapable of working together in a common political space. In a world where most as-yet-undemocratic states are multiethnic – and usually intermixed in a way that makes peaceful dismemberment impossible – one can only hope that successful multination democracies will continue to exist to serve as beacons and role-models for the possibility of democratic tolerance.

That said, it is also true that nobody now really regrets the fact that Norway and Sweden separated early in the twentieth century, or that there are a great many countries in the world today (200 is not necessarily worse than 20, even if it is surely better than 2,000). The fact that some peoples have states of their own, or in which they are the majority, and that other peoples find themselves to be minorities, is more often than not an accident of history. Most states did not form voluntarily the way the USA, Canada and Australia did. Many minority nations have found themselves born into political marriages to which they never consented. Often these marriages have been quite loveless if not violent. The regrettable intolerance and mutual distrust I mentioned a moment ago, then, is sometimes a fact of life. In these situations divorce, or legal secession, would seem only to be making official what is already the case. Secession in some such cases should be legally permissible for much the same reason that the majority of Irish voters finally agreed, in 1995, to make divorce legally permissible – even though, as good Catholics, they also strongly prefer united families.[11]

I mention this as a parting critique of Sunstein's explicit recommendation of the tradition of American constitutionalism to the democratising states of Eastern Europe. It is misleading to think of that tradition as merely a system and rationale for producing good government. It is clear from *The Federalist*, which Sunstein cites throughout, that the aim is also to facilitate the emergence of what we would now call a unified, homogeneous nation. But the contrast between the founding of this young (and for all intents and purposes) ethnically homogeneous state,[12] and the refounding of Eastern European states could not be more stark. The latter, for the most part, include distinct national minority groups that have no intention of assimilating into the majority culture and language.[13] A truly democratic refounding of these states (something that in most cases did *not* take place) would have to take account of this, and their constitutions would ideally reflect a partnership among peoples as well as among equal citizens.[14] This could come symbolically as a recognition of multinationality in, say, the constitutional preamble, and more concretely in terms of language rights, federal or consociational arrangements, special representation and veto rights, and so on[15]. If such groups insisted on the inclusion of a secession clause it might ideally be thought of as a legitimate hedge against the as-yet unproven democratic good will of the majority nation. One problem with recommending the American constitutional tradition for these states is that it strengthens the hand of majority national groups that have often oppressed their minorities in the name of universal norms. Nothing, in short, could be more inappropriate than encouraging nationalist Slovak or Serb leaders to treat their states as 'melting pots'. It is not for nothing that the more common metaphor in that part of the world is 'powder keg'.

## The secession reference to the Supreme Court of Canada: discovering a constitutional procedure when the text itself is silent

Further light was shed on the question of the appropriateness of a secession clause in the constitution of a democratic multination state when the Supreme Court of Canada considered the issue in a Reference, in August 1998. Not long after the federalist side won a narrow victory in the October 1995 secessionist referendum in Quebec (in other words, shortly after the federalists almost lost the referendum!), the Canadian federal Minister of Justice formally sought the Supreme Court's view on whether the unilateral secession of Quebec is legal under Canadian or international law. Like almost all other constitutions, the written text of the Canadian constitution is silent on the issue of secession. The Court made it clear, however, that in its view 'The Constitution is more than a written text. It embraces the entire global system of rules and principles which govern the exercise of constitutional authority.' These rules and principles 'emerge from an understanding of the constitutional text itself, the historical context, and previous judicial interpretations of constitutional meaning' (para. 32). And with these in mind the Court produced a rich discussion of constitutional norms and procedures that should govern any attempt by Quebec to secede from Canada. In a very real sense it 'wrote' a secession clause into the Constitution. Although the terms and procedures it recommends are incomplete in many respects – since the Court deliberately shies away from controversial issues it considers better left to politicians – they nevertheless gained considerable legitimacy when both the federal government and the Parti Québécois government in power in Quebec broadly endorsed the Court's opinion.

There is not space here to look at the Reference in detail. What is worth noting here, however, is the way the Court attempts to balance several sometimes conflicting political values in order to judge the compatibility of secession with the 'Canadian tradition' of democracy, constitutionalism and federalism. In the main, I believe its arguments are broadly in line with what I have argued in this chapter, especially in its emphasis on the rule of law, its insistence that democracy is more than 'a system of simple majority rule' (para. 76), and the clear understanding that constitutionalism involves much more than a set of precommitment strategies (although the judges quite explicitly make use of historical accounts of the motives of the framers of the Constitution; e.g., in sec. III(2)). More specifically, the judges argue that

> In our view, there are four fundamental and organizing principles of the Constitution which are relevant to addressing the question before us (although this enumeration is by no means exhaustive): federalism; democracy; constitutionalism and the rule of law; and respect for minorities.
>
> (para. 32)

In another passage the judges' Opinion clarifies that 'respect for minorities' means respect for minority *rights* (para. 49). It also notes that 'These defining principles function in symbiosis. No single principle can be defined in isolation from the others, nor does any one principle trump or exclude the operation of any other' (para. 49). In the ensuing discussion of these four principles it emphasises, among other things, the essential link between Canada's choice of a federal system and the aspirations of the French-speaking minority that forms a majority in Quebec (para. 59); its belief that 'democracy in any real sense of the word cannot exist without the rule of law', that 'To be accorded legitimacy, democratic institutions must rest, ultimately, on a legal foundation' (para. 67); and that the requirement of enhanced majorities to achieve constitutional change is justified in part to protect the interests of minorities that would be affected by the change.

For the purposes of the issues discussed in this chapter, the Court's final opinion on the Reference questions is less interesting than the considerations it believes are relevant for its arguments. The Court concludes, to nobody's surprise, that there is no right for Quebec to secede *unilaterally* in Canadian law (or in international law, though I am not discussing that issue here). Most observers (including, presumably, the federal Minister of Justice who made the Reference) predicted this conclusion, since the secession of Quebec would involve changing a number of clauses in the Constitution that require the support of all of the provinces and the federal government. The Court's argument, however, is much more sophisticated and far-reaching than this: it believes that unilateral secession would violate *all four* of the fundamental guiding principles it had identified, not just the formal amending formula. But even more, the Court chose to go beyond the narrow, specific questions it was asked and to pronounce upon the processes that would make legitimate or illegitimate an attempt by either the Quebec government to secede or the Canadian government to resist Quebec's attempt to secede. Here the Court argues that 'A clear majority vote in Quebec on a clear question in favour of secession would confer democratic legitimacy on the secession initiative which all of the other participants in Confederation would have to recognize'. They refuse to spell out what would constitute a 'clear question' and what level of support would qualify as a 'clear majority',[16] but they are nevertheless quite clear in indicating that the democratic legitimacy of such a result would require the federal government to negotiate secession in good faith.[17]

It is significant that the highest constitutional court of the third oldest federation in the world has ruled that a legal process for secession is not only *consistent* with democratic federalism, it is actually *required* by it. But it is also worth highlighting some of the shortcomings of its interpretation, considered as a substitute for a fair and just secession clause. As noted already, they do not specify what would count as a clear majority (though they hint strongly that a qualified majority would be appropriate for such a radical change that goes against the will of minorities)[18] or a clear question (although almost all observers recognise that the question in the 1995 referendum was anything but clear).[19] They also say little about who should be at the negotiating table, what would count as negotiating in good faith, and what would happen if negotiations broke down despite the fact that both sides felt they were negotiating in good faith. This is not to criticise the Court. On the contrary: there is good reason to want judges to shy away from pronouncing on such issues.

Within a year and a half of the Supreme Court's Opinion, the federal government of Canada introduced legislation to Parliament that, in effect, took up the challenge that the Court had left to elected politicians; namely, the specification of what would count as a 'clear majority' and a 'clear question'. This legislation (the 'Clarity Act') does not push very far beyond the parameters and justifications given by the Court, and it quite conspicuously refuses to name a figure for what would constitute a clear majority. It does, however, provide a relatively transparent procedure and a definite timeline for the federal government's pronouncing upon these issues. The House of Commons would have to indicate whether it thought a referendum question was clear within 30 days of its being adopted by a provincial legislature; that is, well before the end of a referendum campaign. And if the House judged that the question 'would not result in the clear expression of the will of the population of that province on whether the province should cease to be part of Canada', then the Clarity Act would forbid the Government of Canada to enter into negotiations 'on the terms on which [the] province might cease to be part of Canada'. For good measure, the Act also gives an indication of two kinds of question which would *not* be considered clear for the purpose of initiating negotiations on secession: namely, questions focusing merely on a mandate to negotiate without 'soliciting a direct expression of the will' to actually secede; and a question that 'envisages other possibilities in addition to secession' such as a renewed political and economic partnership with Canada. In effect, this clause indicates that the federal government would not be permitted to negotiate secession on the basis of Yes victories with questions of the sort used in either 1980 or 1995 by the Parti Québécois governments in Quebec. The Clarity Act also requires the House of Commons to pronounce upon whether it believes a 'clear majority' of a province voted in favour of secession, although as I mentioned a moment ago, it does not name a concrete figure. It does, however, indicate that the House would take many factors into account, including not just whether there was a majority of *voters* in favour, but also whether there was a majority of *eligible* voters. And for the determination of the clarity of both the question and the majority, the Act indicates that the House of Commons should consider not only the views of its own members, but also those of opposition parties in the province contemplating secession, as well as formal resolutions by other legislatures in Canada and 'any other views it considers to be relevant'. It is widely understood that this latter expression would include, in the case of another attempted secession by the Government of Quebec, the views of Aboriginal groups who form the majority of inhabitants over much of the sparsely populated land mass throughout the 'grand nord' of the province.

The Clarity Act is, I believe, a pretty good indication of the limit of what a central government can stipulate as its conditions for negotiating secession once a tradition of secessionist politics has become well established in the political culture. It both concedes a right for a province to secede, and also makes it clear that there is no automatic right to secede unilaterally or with a slim majority on a confusing question. And while it does not go significantly beyond the parameters laid down in the Supreme Court Opinion, it does probably make it clearer to the citizens of Quebec and Canada what would happen in the event of a Yes-vote on a secessionist or quasi-secessionist question. In this way it raises the bar ever-so-slightly (though nevertheless, given the potential support for secession in Quebec, significantly), and takes away both uncertainty about what would happen and any false sense of how easy or automatic secession would be with a narrow victory. In so doing, it may well discourage future nationalist governments in Quebec from calling secessionist referenda (since opinion polls have almost never shown a majority – let alone a *clear* majority – in favour of secession when a clear question is asked), or at least make it more difficult politically for them to ask deliberately confusing, vague or ambiguous questions. That said, measures such as those proposed by the Clarity Act would provide relatively little deterrent to secession or secessionist politics in many other states, especially those without long democratic traditions, where alienation from the larger state by a minority group is more complete.

Taken together the Canadian Supreme Court's Opinion and the Clarity Act still amount to a relatively tepid 'juridification' of secession rules compared to what enlightened groups founding a state might be willing to agree to, or what might be agreed upon during constitutional negotiations in a sort of *quid pro quo* that offered a minority nation significant new powers of autonomy in exchange for entrenching procedures that would make secession difficult. In both such cases, the bar for secession could be pushed higher, and given a more concrete profile (e.g., the requirement of a two-thirds majority in favour, the specification of the exact question to be used, or a stipulation that no more than one referendum on secession could be called in a province within a 15- or 20-year period). Such concrete measure to make secession possible but difficult could be legitimised by an actual agreement between the minority nation or nations and the central government, and they would be in line with a view that secession should be encouraged only when there is just cause (such as systematic oppression of a minority group).[20] The principal effect of such measures in many democratic political cultures would be to discourage minority nationalists from playing secessionist politics in the first place (to encourage them to work for minority national mobilisation and rights within other democratic forums). And this is where we see why judicial interpretation of the sort found recently in Canada can never be thought of as an adequate substitute for an enlightened secession clause agreed to and legitimised in advance. The eventual revelation of an implicit secession clause in the Canadian Constitution in 1998 (along with its clarification in a federal Act in 2000) obviously had no dynamic impact on the decision by democratic Quebec nationalists to begin the pursuit of secession in the 1960s and 1970s. And yet it is secessionist politics, as much as (or even more than) secession itself, that a wise constitutional order in a reasonably just democratic state would want to discourage.

## Conclusion

I have argued that in some states, particularly multination states in which there is a distinct possibility of secessionist politics, it would often be appropriate to have provisions for secession entrenched in the constitution. My principal reasons for this derive not from any enthusiasm for secession but rather because, first, secessionist politics in such states are likely to arise with or without such a clause; second, when they do arise they invite political turmoil and violence, squeeze the amount of political time and energy available for other urgent public concerns, and are unlikely to be resolved in as fair a manner as they would have been with prior ground rules; and third, it is reasonable to think that a fair secession clause could actually serve, in some cases at least, as a deterrent to the formation of secessionist politics rather than as a source of encouragement. The argument of the Supreme Court of Canada goes even further (though I have not tried to reproduce it in any detail here), claiming, in effect, that a democratic approach to secession actually *follows from* an advanced understanding of democratic constitutionalism, the rule of law, federalism and minority rights.

In short, it would often be reasonable, fair and wise for democratic peoples founding or reforming a state to agree to include a secession clause in their constitution. No other reason than this should be necessary to show that secession can be democratic – even if the decision to secede would often be, like many other democratic decisions, regrettable.

## Notes

1 For defences of this general view see Beran 1984, Nielsen 1993, Philpott 1994, Wellman 1995 and Copp 1997.
2 For a concise and devastating critique of the direct link between democracy and secession, see Buchanan 1998.
3 Jennings 1956, p. 56 (cited in Moore 1998); Barry 1983, p. 161; Moore 1998, p. 134; Derriennic 1995, pp. 97–102.
4 This rejection of majority rule as the fundamental principle of constitutional democracy is, in a sense, the starting point for all of the chapters in this volume.
5 I do discuss some of the forms a just constitutional secession clause could take in Norman 1998, pp. 50–55.
6 For an excellent discussion of the idea of causal mechanisms in political psychology see Elster 1993.
7 A two-thirds majority requirement for a vote on secession is a feature of one of the world's only explicit secession procedures, in the Constitution of St Kitts-Nevis, a microstate consisting of two islands in the Caribbean. In 1998 a majority, but less than two-thirds, of the voters in Nevis voted to secede and the referendum therefore failed. I am not arguing that a democratic secession procedure would have a two-thirds majority requirement, but only that it would make secession more difficult than 50-per-cent-plus-1 on a question drawn up by the secessionists themselves.
8 The United Nations Charter, Article 1(2), states that a central purpose of the organization is to 'develop friendly relations among nations based on respect for the principle of equal rights and self-determination of peoples'. Articles 55, 73 and 76(1) confirm this principle as do a number of subsequent UN resolutions. While this principle was invoked during the period of decolonisation, most experts agree that it does not imply a legal right of secession. The 1970 Declaration on Friendly Relations makes clear that this principle shall not 'be construed as authorizing or encouraging any action which would dismember or impair, totally or in part, the territorial integrity or political unity of sovereign and independent States', so long as they have governments 'representing the whole people belonging to the territory without distinction as to race, creed or colour'. See Buchheit 1978, Eastwood 1993 and Thornberry 1989.
9 As I shall discuss, the Supreme Court of Canada ruled in 1998 that the Government of Canada would have a constitutional obligation to negotiate the secession of Quebec if a clear majority in the province voted to secede in a referendum with a clear question. Nevertheless, the Court ruled against the legality of a *unilateral* secession under either Canadian or international law.
10 See, e.g., J.S. Mill's horrific description of the legal bondage of wives in England until the mid-nineteenth century in *The Subjection of Women*.

11 For a much more elaborate argument for why the secession of groups without 'just cause' should sometimes be allowed as a regrettable consequence of constitutionalising secession, see Norman 1998, pp. 50–56.

12 Obviously, I am thinking of the 'official view' of the founding of the American federation, involving a predominately Anglo-Saxon political class. African slaves and American Indians do not receive a lot of attention in the Constitution or in *The Federalist Papers* which provide its most influential defence.

13 For a clear discussion of the political relevance of the distinction between ethnic immigrant groups of the sort found in the USA, and national minorities, see Kymlicka 1995, ch. 2. For detailed discussion of interethnic relations in a number of Eastern and Central European states, as well as reflections on what they can learn from Western democracies, see Opalski 1998 and Opalski and Kymlicka 2001.

14 See Chapter 4 by Fossas in this volume for further discussion of the relations and tensions between concerns for equality of citizens, federal subunits, and 'founding peoples'.

15 For a survey of relations and tensions between minority rights and common citizenship, see Kymlicka and Norman 2000.

16 In its summary of its response to Question 1, the Court writes: 'The obligations identified by the Court are binding obligations under the Constitution. However, it will be for the political actors to determine what constitutes "a clear majority on a clear question" in the circumstances under which a future referendum vote may be taken.'

17 'the conduct of the parties [in negotiations following a clear referendum victory for the secessionist side in Quebec] assumes primary constitutional significance. The negotiation process must be conducted with an eye to the constitutional principles we have outlined, which must inform the actions of *all* the participants in the negotiation process. Refusal of a party to conduct negotiations in a manner consistent with constitutional principles and values would seriously put at risk the legitimacy of that party's assertion of its rights, and perhaps the negotiation process as a whole.' (secs 94–95 of The Reference.)

18 See, e.g., secs 77, 87.

19 Here is the question posed by the Parti Québécois government in the referendum of October 1995: '*Do you agree that Quebec should become sovereign, after having made a formal offer to Canada for a new economic and political partnership, within the scope of the bill respecting the future of Quebec and of the agreement signed on June 12, 1995?*' Yes or No. Intense debate in the Quebec National Assembly could not add the word 'country' after the word 'sovereign', presumably because the majority PQ government knew full well that polls consistently show that support for Quebec being 'sovereign' is often 20 per cent higher than support for it becoming a 'sovereign country'. The bill referred to in the question is a long piece of legislation that calls for a declaration of independence if the offer of partnership is refused. And the agreement of 12 June is one between the leaders of the three nationalist parties in Quebec. Polls indicated that more than a quarter of Yes voters believed that Quebec would remain in Canada and continue to send representatives to the Parliament in Ottawa after a Yes victory.

20 Again, for a general defence of the so-called Just-Cause theory of secession, see Norman 1998 and Buchanan 1998.

## References

Barry, Brian (1983, 1991) 'Self-Government Revisited', in *Democracy and Power*. Oxford: Oxford University Press.

Bauböck, Rainer (1999) 'Why Secession is Not Like Divorce', in *Nationalism and Internationalism in the Post-Cold War Era*, edited by Kjell Goldmann, Ulf Hannerz and Charles Westin. London: UCL Press.

Beran, Harry (1984) 'A Liberal Theory of Secession', *Political Studies* 32.

Buchanan, Allen (1991) *Secession: The Morality of Political Divorce from Fort Sumter to Lithuania and Quebec*. Boulder, Col.: Westview Press.

Buchanan, Allen (1998) 'Democracy and Secession', in *National Self-Determination and Secession*, edited by M. Moore. Oxford: Oxford University Press.

Buchheit, Lee (1978) *Secession: The Legitimacy of Self-Determination*. New Haven, Conn.: Yale University Press.

Copp, David (1997) 'Democracy and Communal Self-Determination', in *The Morality of Nationalism*, edited by J. McMahan and R. McKim. New York: Oxford University Press.

Derriennic, Jean-Pierre (1995) *Nationalisme et démocratie*. Montreal: Boréal.

Eastwood, Lawrence (1993) 'Secession: State Practice and International Law After the Dissolution of the Soviet Union and Yugoslavia', *Duke Journal of Comparative and International Law* 3.

Elster, Jon (1993) *Political Psychology*. Cambridge: Cambridge University Press.

Kymlicka, Will (1995) *Multicultural Citizenship: A Liberal Theory of Minority Rights*. Oxford: Oxford University Press.

Kymlicka, Will and Wayne Norman (eds) (2000) *Citizenship in Diverse Societies*. Oxford: Oxford University Press.

Moore, Margaret (1997) 'On National Self-Determination', *Political Studies* 45.

Moore, Margaret (ed.) (1998) *National Self-Determination and Secession*. Oxford: Oxford University Press.

Nielsen, Kai (1993) 'Secession: The Case of Quebec', *Journal of Applied Philosophy* 10.

Norman, Wayne (1998) 'The Ethics of Secession as the Regulation of Secessionist Politics', in *National Self-Determination and Secession*, edited by M. Moore. Oxford: Oxford University Press.

Opalski, Magda (ed.) (1998) *Managing Diversity in Plural Societies: Minorities, Migration and Nation-building in Post-Communist Europe*. Ottawa: Forum Eastern Europe.

Opalski, Magda and Will Kymlicka (eds) (2001) *Can Liberal Pluralism be Exported?* Oxford: Oxford University Press.

Philpott, Daniel (1994) 'In Defense of Secession', *Ethics* 105.

*Reference re Secession of Quebec* [1998] 2 S.C.R. 217 (Supreme Court of Canada).

Sunstein, Cass (1991) 'Constitutionalism and Secession', *University of Chicago Law Review* 58.

Thornberry, Patrick (1989) 'Self-Determination, Minorities, Human Rights: A Review of International Instruments', *International and Comparative Law Quarterly* 38.

Wellman, Christopher (1995) 'A Defense of Secession and Political Self-Determination', *Philosophy and Public Affairs* 24.

# Part III

# National pluralism and the European Union

# 6 National plurality within single statehood in the European Union

*Carlos Closa*

## Introduction

Discussions on multiculturalism, national plurality and citizenship turn often towards European Union citizenship. This 'new' institution appeals simultaneously as a test and as a possible solution for some of the most compelling questions raised within other settings. And yet, EU citizenship offers more unresolved issues than answers to demands. Debates on the outstanding issue of defining the contours of plurinational states exemplify this situation. On the one hand, EU citizenship may be regarded as a possible device that provides a more diffuse institutional alternative for deriving rights and identity than the one provided by statehood (of member states). However, reality does not match expectations; in its current stage of development, the contribution of EU citizenship for the eventual settlement of issues of national plurality is mainly symbolic and, in practical terms, prospective rather than effective and current. This situation allows therefore a prospective standpoint in which normative arguments precede and enlighten institutional constructions.

This chapter focuses on the exploration of the issue of national plurality within member states. By national plurality is meant a well-known situation in which a state might gather several national communities. In order to substantiate a discussion on the eventual role of EU citizenship in facing issues of plural statehood or minority nationalism within the EU, this chapter examines EU citizenship and some other EU institutional arrangements. The first section describes EU citizenship as a manifestation of post-national citizenship. If traditionally citizenship moved in the conceptual environment of the nation-state, EU citizenship has to be mainly understood within the context of redefinition of traditional links between right and identity, on the one hand, and statehood, on the other. Thus, the positive juridical statute of EU citizenship becomes possible by separating the statutes (and concepts) of nationality (linked to sovereign member states) and citizenship (understood mainly as a set of rights). The legal and theoretical construction of EU citizenship is consistent with deductive theoretical notions of citizenship, specifically, with cosmopolitanism. An inquiry on the claims or empirical requirements that can be fitted while keeping normative coherence follows in the second section. Specifically, this section spells out the theoretical requirements to make compatible the foundation of EU citizenship with the claims of existing national plurality. The EU may offer general guarantists provisions of minority rights and general institutional arrangements for sub-state territorial units. This second option, that is reviewed in the third section, does not however resolve in a fully satisfactory way the claims of territorial units. Institutional arrangements for regions and sub-state entities within the EU open up their structure for political opportunity and legitimise some of their political claims. But so far, the emergence of a 'Europe of the regions' is far from being a reality and, paradoxically, the EU has had an unintended standardising effect that reduces salience of claims of differential nationalism. Finally, the fourth section turns attention towards the effects of the institutional configuration of EU multilevel governance on individuals' self on the assumption that institutions do not simply crystallise pre-existing social and political demands; by their very existence, they become references for identity.

## EU citizenship: the post-national model

EU citizenship can be counted as a manifestation of deep changes of institutions of modernity posed by logics such as regional integration and/or globalisation that during the second half of the twentieth century have induced a reconfiguration of nation-states. While the classical theory of the state substantiated a canonical notion of political domination around the triad of a people, a territory and (a single) sovereignty, European integration (as much as the logic of globalisation) induces at least a relativisation of these three elements.

Changes affect, first, the very notion of citizenship, around which the reflection on the human condition has been lately organised. In the republican foundation of the modern concept in the nineteenth century, the notion of citizenship seemed more closely connected with a participatory dimension and the issue of political rights. The revision of Marshall underlined the salience of social rights within this construction and, in parallel, placed citizenship as the central piece for political development.

The turn induced by the new context of globalisation points towards more complex forms of articulation between rights and identity. In particular, one of the more influencing developments is the loosening of the tight link between rights and national identity constructed by the ideology of the nation-state. Globalisation motivates two simultaneous processes: discourses at the global level and valorisation of local cultures (glocalisation), both as sources of construction of identity, rights and, lately, statutes such as citizenship. Within the globalised context, human rights gain currency as an alternative basis for individuals' status, international institutional designs are slowly becoming stronger and even at the state level the enlargement of fundamental rights to all legal residents reflects this universalistic turn. And also local communities find the suitable situation for the assertion of the moral value of their idiosyncratic features.

The institution of EU citizenship has been constructed on this changing moral and political background. However, realism suggests a lowering of expectations: despite enrichment by legal, political and sociological doctrines, EU citizenship is, first and foremost, a juridical statute composed by a set of rights. Within these rights, three different categories can be distinguished. First, some rights are explicitly constructed as such citizenship rights (i.e. EU citizenship provisions). A second group of rights derive from Treaty provisions policy-oriented (for instance, social policy). Finally, the third category would be constructed around some provisions (for instance, social and economic cohesion). In contrast to the former, there may be discussions on whether these Treaty provisions construct rights or not.

The creation of this positive juridical statute relies on political and technical mechanisms. On the political side, the appeal to citizens' rights has become a powerful legitimising tool for the development of a new polity (the EU) (Lyons 1996) and some of its specific policies. On the side of the juridical technique, it has made possible the breakdown between nationality and citizenship. By nationality is meant a juridical statute that expresses the link between a state and an individual. It should be noticed that this concept is not exactly symmetric with the sociological notion of nationhood that expresses also belonging. While nationality sanctions in positive legal terms belonging to a state, a sovereign form of public power, nationhood refers to a human collective, regardless of its quality as sovereign power. Nationality and nationhood are not coterminous, although in nation-states there is an assumption of the superposition between both. The progressive affirmation of plurinationalism (short of claiming full statehood) within states has lately given sense to this distinction.

On this background, the juridical statute of EU citizenship reflects an ongoing process of decoupling (within states as much as above them) between rights (citizenship) and nationality (as the exclusivist juridical entitlement for rights). This process has been labelled post-national citizenship, in a fortunate coincidence among scholars from different intellectual disciplines. Sociologists such as Yasemin Soysal use the term in order to describe *a new model of membership, anchored in the universalistic rights of personhood, where identity and rights, the two elements of citizenship, are decoupled* (Soysal 1994). She draws on empirical evidence to state that 'performance' more than 'belonging' is becoming the essential element to define participation (Soysal 1996). Similarly, legal theorists such as Luigi Ferrajoli have argued that, in logical (and moral) terms, personhood is an alternative statute to citizenship in order to anchor rights. In normative terms, he postulates the revalorisation of the statute of 'legal personality' as an alternative statute to national citizenship (Ferrajoli 1993). From this, a new taxonomy of rights *rationae personae* is constructed where the basic Marshall assumption of the attribution of civil, political and social rights to citizens is put into question (Ferrajoli 1999).

In both cases, the theoretical constructions are substantiated (or confirmed) by empirical evidence which, in a very simple wording, could be summarised in the following statement: modern constitutionalism advances in granting rights (fundamental and others) to almost all residents (regardless of nationality) and only political rights are restricted for citizens. Philosophers and political theorist such as Habermas or Ferry have provided the theoretical normative argument to base this development.

The evaluation of the impact of this development on the traditional moral comprehension of the nation-state is necessarily ambiguous. On the one hand, the sources for the re-configuration of national citizenship are not restricted to the ones provided by national communities: international law, knowledge of other cultures, and so on, have nurtured discussions on identity with new points of reference. But, on the other hand, these changes derive also from both the logical development of moral requirements for the statute of (national) citizenship (such as equality) and discursive processes of (national) democracy. Democratic discussions on citizenship lead towards the accommodation of rights whose source may be in the global context. Thus, what is induced is a redefinition of the moral comprehension of the nation-state.

What has not changed so dramatically in this new setting is that nation-state authorities (political and judicial) are still the ones in charge of guaranteeing this decoupling. States are still the condition for the validity of rights. Despite the growing availability of institutional alternatives (such as the EU itself), nation-states remain still the main frame for the validity of rights, and human rights have not yet displaced fundamental rights in contemporary constitutionalism. The paradox is well expressed in the view of the EU as an adaptative response of the nation-state in order to retain its sovereignty.

Leaving aside shortcomings, scholars are increasingly coincident in identifying EU citizenship as a form of post-national citizenship (Bauböck 1997; Shaw 1997). The provisions guaranteeing member states identity and citizenship reinforce the profile of a statute detached of identitarian substrate whose options for development have been reviewed elsewhere (Closa 1997). A second influence impinges upon the future configuration of EU citizenship: the relative loosening of the assumptions of modernity that place on reason the source of deductive construction of rights. More specifically, the logic of globalisation induces a relativism deriving from the valorisation of local and regional cultures in which rights might be grounded. In the words of U. Beck, this logic introduces a re-formulation of the foundation of first modernity around questions such as what does tolerance mean? What do human rights imply for different cultures? And who does guarantee human rights in the post nation-state world (Beck 1999)? This forms the background for an inquiry on the eventual relationship between EU institutions (such as citizenship) and national plurality in single statehood.

## Contours of the relationship between national plurality and EU citizenship

Citizenship is, first and foremost, a word, a concept with an enormously rich connotation and denotation: rights, identity, difference, inclusion are part of its connotation. Since the work of Marshall and in a special way in the 1980s and 1990s, it has also become the central concept for reflection for the human condition and the problems related. Poverty, belonging, democracy, institutional designs and rules are just a small number of the large number of issues that can be tackled under this concept. An agreement on the plurality of connotations and applications of the concept opens the path to set the assumption for the following. Citizenship is a concept which presents the characteristic methodological problem of incommensurability, that is ad hoc applications of the same word but with asymmetrical meanings in different settings and discourses. Moreover, the validity of a concept is exhausted when used with a polemist or programmatic bias. Thus, delimiting theoretical and practical requirements becomes a compelling necessity.

## Theoretical requirements

The proper theoretical construction of a notion of EU citizenship that might eventually frame the treatment of national plurality should satisfy claims from two different logical origins; deductive and inductive. The notion of EU citizenship should be compatible with a *deductive* theoretical construction since these enlighten on outstanding normative issues. In particular, it seems that cosmopolitanism provides a consistent theoretical framework since it is coherent with the post-national model designed by EU citizenship.

A priori, it seems that there exists theoretical coherence between EU foundation and the requirements of minority nationalism. EU citizenship has been designed as a statute whose referent is states' nationality or, in other words, the meaning of EU citizenship is releasing rights from their tight link to state nationality. Precisely because of that, it might be regarded as a useful institution to fit claims that equally try to lose the connection between rights and nationality in favour of the promotion of rights of non-state nations. In principle, the coincidence of their antagonism to privileged statehood nationality seems to bring close EU citizenship rights and the rights demanded for the recognition of sub-state groups rights.

Are these two developments compatible from the point of view of the normative foundations of each? The implicit generalisation of nation-state rights for any national of a member state meant by EU citizenship derives from a solid individualistic grounding of these rights. The story of rights within the EU (owing probably to its market origin) refers systematically to individuals. Thus, EU citizenship becomes an affirmation of individuals' rights *vis-à-vis* rights' attachment to a specific group difference defined by statehood nationality.

This spells out a normative requirement for fitting rights of minorities: to keep the basic character of EU citizenship. Its foundation, the basic principle behind its development, has been the prohibition of discrimination. Thus, the normative requirement is an avoidance of forms of discrimination *formulated as rights*. Still, this does not mean a normative rejection of these claims but rather they re-address towards more suitable institutional settings.

*Practical demands*

Apart from these normative requirements, practical (inductive) demands require close scrutiny. In some instances, *inductive theoretical* notions have polluted the theorisation on EU citizenship. In other words, the notion of EU citizenship has been affected by attempts to translate bits and pieces of national configurations of citizenship. Thus, for instance, the idea of the 'conceptual heritage' focus (Shaw 1997) picks up elements for the reconstruction of the concept of EU citizenship, even though their sources are national concepts and, in this form, they tend to reconstruct the nation-state (and, implicitly, associating the European polity with a State). Releasing EU citizenship from the nation-state model is a compelling demand since each national configuration reflects a specific set of cleavages and historical processes. Moreover, the nation-state model of citizenship anchors the notion within the limits of the traditional conception of the state. For instance, supporters of minority nations' claims identify some of these limits: the marginalisation of plurality in the regulation of the 'ethical' national dimension, a monist conception of the *demos*, and the application of functional criteria in the territorial division of powers based on the standardising logic of subsidiarity (Requejo 1998).

The institution required is one consistent with a normative framework theoretically established but also informed by solid practical requirements. The inductive requirements examined here are those of national pluralism. Therefore, the objective is the identification of the eventual contribution of EU citizenship to (the accommodation) of existing national plurality within the EU and some of its member states. Some authors perceive EU citizenship as an instrument providing a greater potential for the citizens of the different *demos* of plurinational states on two conditions. First, there is a regulation of a number of rights that guarantee the recognition of existing national plurality; and, second, it ensures a level of self-government for the different national groups in proportion to this recognition (Requejo 1998: 47). Therefore, what is required is the coherence of this development, that is recognition, with the theoretical foundation of EU citizenship.

But it may be deceptive to think of national pluralism as a situation that presents clear demands. Running away from an essentialist definition of nation or culture, it seems that the factic situation of current minorities results from long-standing cleavages that have survived historical processes of integration developed by nation-states. There exist at least three different groups that can fit in this situation within the EU context. There exist, first, national minorities within current member states whose constitutional systems (however unsatisfactorily) are supposed to be democratic and respectful of rights of minorities. Second, forthcoming Eastern member states; they contain national minorities often linked to surrounding nation-states. Their former totalitarian past and creeping nationalism have raised some fears of mistreatment of these. These Eastern applicant states have been the object of scrutiny and debate on the standards guaranteed to their respective national minorities. In fact, some provisions that seek to guarantee minority nations' rights have been developed having in mind these applicant states. Finally, a third situation, which is not normally treated under the same label, is the position of non-territorial minorities, such as Gypsies or Muslims. While the former two may find accommodation through specific territorial institutional designs, the third group seems to challenge this option.

These differences put a limit to universalistic EU provisions or single institutional arrangements. In agreement with the theoretical requirement of consistency, EU citizenship can be the basis for recognition and guarantee of rights of national minorities. The precise contours are outlined in the following paragraphs. Before this, a word of caution is included: EU citizenship should not be considered the 'universal solution' for any kind of problem. Universal provisions on fundamental rights and other EU institutions complete the instruments for accommodation of national plurality.

## The contours of eventual provisions on minority nations

However, EU citizenship offers some reduced possibilities for framing rights available for recognition of non-state nations' rights. These are located in the form of guarantist provisions (i.e. provisions that guarantee an individual freedom) rather than the more classical 'empowerment' rights. Basically, this guarantist approach is contained by the after-war system of protection of minorities that has been based on a universalistic conception of human rights. Within this conception, the notion of equality plays the role of minority protection by guaranteeing rights without discrimination. Several international covenants and declarations adopt this view (International Pact on Civil and Political Rights (art. 27); Final Act of the Helsinki Conference (principle VII); UNO Declaration on the rights of persons belonging to religious, ethnic, linguistic and national minorities and European Charter on minority and regional languages). Only the 1990 Paris Charter (drafted with an eye on Eastern transitions to democracy) marks a move towards a collective conception that is interested not only in protection but also on promotion through positive discrimination (Decaux 1998).

Within the EU, there exist some provisions that portray a similar guarantist approach based on equality of the rights of persons and non-discrimination. In this line can be mentioned the Protocol of the Treaty of Amsterdam on the guarantee for minority religions. Also, the Draft Charter on Fundamental Rights of the EU (whose provisions are in many respects absolutely insufficient) picks up protection of minorities within the general guarantee of equality and non-discrimination (arts. 20 and 21). More clearly, the Treaty of Amsterdam included a new provision (art. 13 Treaty of the European Community) for combating discrimination because of racial and ethnic origin, religion or belief among other criteria. The strength of the legal commitment imposed upon member states and the null capability to escape them may explain the comparative weakness of EU mechanisms for minority protection *vis-à-vis* international ones.

The content of these guarantist provisions should not advance further than the protection of rights and institutional arrangements for minority nations already recognised within the domestic level. Solid practical and theoretical arguments back this position. First, the already mentioned asymmetry between non-state communities puts a practical limit to general clauses. The kind of rights demanded by each minority nation are context-specific. These result from specific historical processes of configuration of each of the member states and their respective settlement (or lack of) of diverse cleavages. Thus, the recognition and guarantee for rights of national minorities may be fitted within EU citizenship but differentiated treatment proportional to recognition must be the result of domestic arrangements. The former section develops further the contradictory effect of EU institutions for differential treatment of territorial units.

Second, there exists a limit to the legitimacy of the EU to act in that direction. In other words, EU citizenship could not create a new empowerment surpassing existing ones within concrete member states since the condition of legitimacy of EU citizenship has been the respect of nation-states' own configurations of citizenship. While the value of national citizenship is generally taken for granted, the affirmation of EU citizenship clashes with communitarian affirmation of the value of pre-existing nation-state communities. The communities meant are of course those of states and the influence of this communitarian trend in the design of EU citizenship can be detected in the guarantist provisions attached to it: the Protocol on nationality annexed to the Maastricht Treaty and article 17.1 of the Treaty of

Amsterdam. This latter raised to the level of command the implicit character of the statute: *citizenship of the Union shall complement and shall not substitute national citizenship*. Thus, a condition of legitimacy of EU citizenship is that it cannot explicitly be used as an instrument to erode national citizenship. The process of right creation within the EU must currently satisfy certain conditions for its legitimacy. And these conditions (for instance, a unanimous agreement on constitutional change) may be contradictory with theoretical constructions, whatever its goodness. More precisely, if the issue of recognition were not previously settled at the national level, its constitutionalisation at the EU level (impossible at practical level) would create a source of legitimacy and legality overruling member states, so far the legitimate contracting parties. This overruling (which may be perceived as legitimate by some) has, however, different implications for different constituencies in different member states.

This does not mean a deprivation of value for EU provisions although their meaning requires a delimitation of its validity or effects for different levels of authority. Targets are central governments and European institutions. For the latter, guarantist provisions may be understood in the sense that Union activity must not imply a discrimination for minorities, an interpretation fully consistent with the requirements spelt out above. It might be also understood as a command for Union behaviour to direct its cultural, political and economic life; a kind of condition. Some actions and policies, such as the creation of the European Bureau for Minority Languages, go in this direction. As far as they built on pre-existing recognition and they do not build new entitlements, they are perfectly legitimate within the EU context. Other provisions, such as the extension of EU citizenship guarantee to use the own language (that is currently refers to communications with EU institutions) might be enlarged to fit a guarantee of the use of minority nations' languages. However, this development may clash with practical difficulties (the exponential increase in the number of EU working languages).

Second, guarantees have an undoubted value *vis-à-vis* the central institutions of member states and their eventual undemocratic tendencies. The prospects for the accession of a number of new democracies with large national minorities justified the elaboration of political criteria for membership, being one of these that the candidate country demonstrates 'respect for and protection of minorities'. Later on, Accession Partnerships included concrete targets on minority protection for several applicant states (Slovakia, Czech Republic, Latvia, Estonia, Hungary, Bulgaria and Romania). Copenhagen criteria did not have legal binding force, even though the Treaty of Amsterdam transposed all of them (but the one on minority protection) as primary EU law (Toggenburg 2000). The so-called Eastern clause, that is the possibility of scrutinising the application of the principles of democracy and respect for human rights by member states, exemplifies this turn. In this second modality, provisions to guarantee rights of national minorities should progressively move under the control of the European Court of Justice (ECJ) rather than only under Council decisions.

In any case, these general provisions provide a general framework of reference but the satisfaction of the claims for recognition of minority nations within EU member states depends rather on specific institutional arrangements that empower these groups. The next section discusses some of the features of these arrangements on the assumption that they only may be applied to territorially defined nations.

## Institutional arrangements for sub-state entities within the EU

The contribution of the EU and the integration process to the recognition of claims of minority nations has been relatively important although indirect and it has acted in a twofold direction. On the one hand, the EU provides new institutional arrangements for sub-state entities and strengthens pre-existing ones within member states. On the other hand and in parallel, the integration process (similarly to globalisation) enhances the legitimacy of claims for self-government. The following two subsections review both of these dimensions.

### Institutional opening-up of the structure of political opportunities

The EU has enlarged the structure of political opportunities by providing a widened institutional setting that, nevertheless, has had a double effect: institutional reinforcement and homogenisation of treatment. The reinforcement effect came about, first, through regional policy and the conscious drive towards partnership embedded within it. In the late 1980s, the EU Commission (supported by regional authorities) sponsored joint co-management of EU, state and regional authorities in steering the programmes of the regional policy. It is debatable whether the implicit intention was exclusively an increase of efficiency of EU policy through joint management but the undoubted effect has been that EU regional policy has pressed towards the development of regional authorities and even the creation of this level in states such as Portugal. During the 1980s and 1990s, it became a commonplace to refer to the emergence of a Europe of the Regions having in mind simultaneously the dilution of nation-states by the integration process and their internal erosion because of the emergence of sub-state powers. More cautious evaluations, however, seem to agree that the Europe of the Regions is a term whose connotation exceeds the mere description of the pattern of relations and institutional configurations generated by EU regional policy. No doubt, regions and sub-state entities have gained importance but a reconfiguration of the predominant political system at a sub-state level seems questionable. Member states are still the main source of power and actors within the EU scene and this signifies both the protagonism of central government as much as that the role of sub-state entities is mediated by national governments. Thus, European integration addresses a model of governance characterised by the interconnection of several administrative levels, the so-called multilevel governance.

Empowerment for sub-state entities through regional policy does not fit perfectly with claims for recognition by minority nations within member states. The main task of EU regional policy has (and still is) been territorial economic development. In consequence, the conception of region for the purposes of EU regional policy followed from economic criteria as much as from political ones. And, therefore, the assumption derived from EU regional policy is the *symmetry* between the so-called regions. This means that resources are made equal for any territorial entity defining itself as region to the effects of the EU regional policy without further consideration of its constitutional standing and the substrate (i.e. national character). To the effects of EU regional policy, political, administrative and financial differences among European regions become secondary in front of economic criteria. EU regional policy empowers regions but it places them at an equal standing.

The effect has been that institutional constructions for regional participation have followed equality of treatment (which is basically an expression of equal treatment for member states) as the organisational criteria. These institutions, more precisely, the Committee of Regions, are the second source for the opening-up of the structure of political opportunities for regions. The Committee seems designed to fit the claims for larger regional participation within the EU. It is made up of representatives of all EU member states regardless of their territorial structure and their national plurality. It thus gathers entities from single-nation and centralised states (such as Denmark) with single-nation federalism (Germany, Austria), plurinational regional states

(Spain, Belgium), and so on. Representatives of local authorities add further heterogeneity, with the final effect that the membership of the Committee might portray the real territorial distribution of power throughout the Union. But certainly, it does not convey the different nature of each level within each member state. Consequently, it could be argued that the effect of institutionalisation of sub-state participation within the EU has led towards a standardising logic that assumes equal treatment for any entity that claims its sub-state level (and has recognition as such by its respective state). This is regardless of their link with a national minority within plurinational member states. Clearly, this status quo might be unsatisfactory for minority nationalism claims (such as, for instance, the Catalan, Basque or Scottish ones), since it imposes a homogenisation that diminishes their political salience and, logically, does not follow from recognition of national difference (although it enhances the political opportunities of the most conscious regions). In a way, the effect resembles the one produced within the Spanish state of autonomies: from an initial specific device for accommodating the claims for self-government of the three minority nations, the logic of the system has produced finally a certain homogenisation.

Similar obstacles for a representative accommodation of sub-state diversity relates to the role of the largely cheered principle of subsidiarity. Within the EU, subsidiarity has been deductively constructed as a guarantist or protective principle for member states *vis-à-vis* centralising efforts and it has been frequently invoked as guarantor of national diversity. In this form, some EU actors interpret it as a principle that, among other things, protects national competencies from homogenising temptations. In parallel, subsidiarity has been instrumental in legitimising claims from sub-state levels of government within member states, in particular in the most centralised states. While this development fits apparently with claims for self-government, it raises some challenges. The principle contains a powerful logical justification in favour of any sub-state entity on the basis of closeness to citizens. Since closeness is a defining feature of lower levels of government, subsidiarity treats equally all of these. But, within plurinational states, the moral justification for self-government derives from cultural or national difference (and not from closeness). In turn, grounding institutional constructions on the federalist principle implies a uniformising logic and it implies a tacit dilution of difference. Thus, the same principle that has been perceived within EU discourse as a guarantee for national difference and empowerment for regions may be seen simultaneously as a threat at the sub-state national level.

The reference to the former two institutional settings for sub-state participation presents a paradox. On the one hand, they enlarge truly the structure of political opportunities for all sub-state entities. On the other hand, they place all of them on equal standing regardless of their link with minority nations or their purely administrative origins. No doubt, sub-state entities based on national difference are keener in using it for enhancing their salience as well, as they pioneer any development along this line.

EU membership projects also affect the domestic institutional configuration of sub-state entities. Subsidiarity seems to have had at least some rhetoric role in member states such as the UK (but, as has been mentioned above, its role is minor if not contradictory in the case of multinational states with a constitutionally consolidated federal or autonomic organisation). And this might be precisely the conclusion: the integration process seems to reinforce the already existing territorial organisation rather than stimulating deep changes (Goetz 1995). National constitutions, that are firmly reaffirmed nowadays as the source of validity and legitimacy of EU membership, are the late source of member states' territorial organisation, and central authorities are highly reticent to accept even implicit changes deriving from the integration process to the domestic Constitutional territorial organisation. In the Spanish case, the government has rebuffed attempts to anchor the subsidiarity principle. Central governments have also been particularly reticent to accept mechanisms for enhancing participation by Autonomous Communities (AC) in EU affairs. On the one hand, the possibility of having a representative of AC sitting at the Council of Ministers taking the place of the Spanish representative, as happens with the German *Länder*. Again, one of the problems posed would be that the place at the Council might be allocated to any of the AC since the criteria would be the impact of the discussed policy on AC competencies. On this background, claims from minority nationalism would lose strength.

## Enlarged ideological resources for minority nationalism

The preceding subsection has described EU institutional arrangements for sub-state entities and the practical effects that they have in the standing of minority nations. These practical effects may or may not generate institutional rearrangements more according with claims of minority nations. But, in any case, they nurture normative and ideological resources. Specifically, the European integration process and EU institutional arrangements strengthen and enlarge the arguments at disposal of minority nationalism (although it does add arguments from a practical origin and not from a normative source). In substantial terms, this means a reinforcement of their claims for self-government in parallel to a reduction of the maximum objective (sovereign statehood).

First of all, European integration provides a practical *confirmation* for some of the normative claims put forward by non-state nationalism. European integration erodes the classical perception of sovereign states born out of the Westphalia system. In particular, it questions *practically* the attributes of sovereign statehood such as impenetrability or unicity. (The practical character of this effect must be underlined because the more doctrinal or theoretical attempts of institutional actors such as the ECJ and the European Parliament to set a foundation for the EU integration process further than member states' sovereignty have been fiercely rebuffed.) Logically, the EU and the integration process challenge also these attributes when applied to the classical subjective referent of sovereignty, the nation. Thus, for instance, the privileged statute traditionally associated with nationality (meaning statehood) yields progressively to the status of EU citizenship. In practical terms, the exclusiveness associated to national belonging is reduced to participation in local elections and few more (albeit meaningful) rights.

Minority nationalism within states targets doctrinally similar definitions of the nation of the state. They attempt to make compatible traditional statehood with plurinationalism and a specific territorial organisation that guarantees self-power of minority nations. The new emerging form of political domination called multilevel governance is coherent and allows the institutional accommodation of the recognition of difference. Minority nationalism finds solid grounds on the several measures of territorial management adopted by states to preserve their own integrity. These comprise decentralised institutions, special representation for regions and particular economic and fiscal measures. This 'new territorial politics' serves well for the reinvention of territory by 'new nationalism' (Keating 1996).

EU institutions and politicians have been particularly receptive towards regional claims since these contribute to enhance EU (and their own) autonomy from the monopoly of political power exercised by national governments. Regions' participation also conveys one of the aims behind the integration process: diffusion of state power. In reference to Spain, it has been mentioned that Catalan and Basque Country regions support the strengthening of European institutions since it erodes the nation-state powers and offers many opportunities for a growing cooperation with other European regions. Their calculation is that, in the long term, the process of political and economic union will lead to the reshaping of the European space on the basis of some coherent and competitive macro-regions (Morata 1996: 153). But the final shape or outcome of the institutional reconfiguration within the EU should not hide the high ideological and rhetorical value of the claim in itself: statements on the emergence of a 'Europe of the Regions' must be cautious ones, since they portray not so much a description of facts but a dogmatic idea to justify an increase in powers for sub-national entities (Borras *et al.* 1994: 1).

A second, derived, ideological resource is the *legitimisation* that the EU provides for the reassertion of minority nationalism claims regarding the configuration of institutions for self-government. Some of the EU induced regional arrangements and principles such as subsidiarity have been mentioned above. In particular the latter, initially constructed as a protective device for states, has contributed to the development of a certain presumption of goodness in favour of regions. Regions' involvement is considered desirable, enriching and even a mechanism for improving the efficiency of policies. It is also portrayed as a greater closeness to citizenship by enlarging the institutional structure for citizens' participation. And, in this sense, regional participation is generally framed within the objective of 'enhancing democracy'. Surprisingly, the presumption of goodness in favour of sub-state entities obviates the fact that this structure of enlarged institutional opportunities for participation favours basically regional executives rather than representative bodies.

Without any doubt, the deeper effect of EU membership and the integration process on the ideological constructions of minority nationalism is the creation of a new political framework for the definition of ultimate objectives. Traditionally, nationalism has aimed to the late target of national independence and self-determination whose concretion is sovereign statehood. The EU induces a redefinition of this scenery. On the one hand, the dilution of classical attributes of statehood implied by EU membership diminishes the symbolic (or real) coercive perception of states by minority nations and this might make less compelling maximum demands for independence. On the other hand, in its current stage of development, EU processes induce a certain degree of realism on the expectations of an independent statute within the EU. Although symbolic presence of a new nation-state would be probably enhanced, real influence and benefit deriving from EU membership would be probably larger within the package deal on membership that a large member state can make. Additionally, the realist perception points towards the prevailing attitude: existing member states will certainly not cherish any move that goes towards an increment in the number of members, moves that may have a demonstration effect within their own territories. Nationalistic movements perceive clearly this lack of receptivity that matches the formerly referred sympathetic attitude towards regions. Thus, nationalism and regionalism find within the EU a more plural context than the classic duality state-region. This has a subtle effect on nationalist discourse and rhetoric. While the EU opens up the structure of political opportunities, it also leads towards a parallel decline in the maximum nationalistic objective of creating independent states (Marks and Llamazares 1995). In fact, minority nationalism within existing member states has often referred to the objective of the construction of a Europe of diversity (Jáuregui 1997).

## Institutions and self: difficulties for fitting multilevel territorial identities

The earlier sections have focused on the institutional opportunities for the participation of minority nations in EU political life. But it should not be overlooked that institutions, further than their positive design, are a meaningful device for individuals' symbolic constructions on their own identities, that is, it may become a significant device for self-construction. As Kymlicka and Norman summarise after a comprehensive survey (Kymlicka and Norman 1994), the citizen is a distilled concept from two key components: rights and identity. The standard perception of the relationship between them assumes that the institution of citizenship stems from a pre-existing identity, as some derivative from a consolidated history and national character. But it may also be sustained that both the practice of freedoms and rights stemming from a certain statute and the policies carried through produce effects on individuals' self-perceptions on themselves and their fellow people. Thus, identity has also a constructivist dimension, as product of the working of institutions.

Scholars apply the same theoretical sequence to EU citizenship. Lacking a repository that could be considered as EU identity, the safe departure point are national identities. These have preceded in time the creation of EU citizenship and, hence, the assumption is that they model and condition any identity associated with EU citizenship and EU policies and institutions. From this standpoint, the issue at stake is how different identities fit within the new institution of EU citizenship and also (taking into account the constructivist dimension referred to above) how the new institution may model selves and identity attached.

More extensively, the argument focuses on how the availability of institutions enlarges and enriches the self of individuals.

Starting from these pre-existing national identities, the significance of EU citizenship differs according to the perceptions of different national groups. Thus, on the one hand, there have existed protective reactions in front of what is perceived as a challenge for national identities. This perception was evident, for instance, in Danish reaction during the ratification of the Treaty of Maastricht. According to the Declaration negotiated by Danish government (that is not an exception to any of the rights of EU citizenship) they feared that it might substitute and eliminate their national citizenship. Empirical precedence of national identities provides a basis for normative preferences: national identities are taken for granted as something good and EU citizenship should not ideally affect these.

On the other hand, EU citizenship provides a complementary identification for those for whom state nationhood does not offer full meaning. Theoretically, it could be assumed that EU citizenship makes more tolerable single statehood within national plurality contexts. Again, this assumption obviates the heterogeneity of situations and the derived diverging views on institutions. Within Spain, for instance, voters of some parties of minority nations perceive EU citizenship as a useful instrument to substitute or eliminate state citizenship. It is an added referential resource against the state. Others perceive it as a *moderating complement* to state citizenship that softens the (hypothetical) pressure put by state on plural identity.

It is this second, milder and tolerant view, the one assumed as referent and model by scholars in order to construct theoretical models fitting several bonds of allegiance; a model of identity that can integrate several and complex sources for self-construction (*nested identities, multilevel identities*). One of these is the concept of multilayered citizenship that is based on the very fact of plurality of self-referents; as Bader writes, we all live with multiple, dynamic and shifting identities, loyalties and commitments (Bader 1999). The model is constructed by reference to different sources of allegiance that have a different origin: for instance, functional identities (stemming from individuals performance in everyday life) or territorial identities. From the point of view interesting here, the different nature of these identities eases their compatibility. In particular, functional identities seem to be easily fitted with primary identities. For instance, consumer identity does seem highly compatible with the national one, as does working identity, and so on. It might be argued that these are weak identities and that is precisely what makes them so manageable. But even so, it seems that, in the absence of strong processes of rationalisation in favour of functional identities, national ones tend to prevail in case of conflict with functional ones. This is demonstrated by the persuasiveness of the 'buy Spanish' (or French or British) campaigns among otherwise conscious consumers.

Applying the model to EU citizenship, the sources for identity construction widen substantially. Functional ones, such as Euro-consumers or Euro-workers, add to the more traditional ones. The source that interests more here is the one attached to different levels of political authority since it relates to the issue of national plurality in single statehood. This has been usually called *multilevel identity* and *multilevel citizenship*, a notion that seeks the accommodation of several territorial layers (being (Meehan 1993) a pioneer in its utilisation referred to the EU). In this way, multilevel identity and citizenship (apart from functional dimensions) is primarily viewed as an accommodation of identities associated with the sub-state, state and supra-state institutional settings.

The new context induces greater complexity in the sources for the formation of identity but this does not imply simultaneously a greater capability of individuals to deal with this complexity. Contrariwise, the view of a harmonic accommodation between levels of identity seems to portray somehow wishful thinking. In fact, there exist large difficulties for fitting multilevel territorial identities within a non-conflictive self. These difficulties derive from the role of institutions: according to Douglas (1986), institutions act as constructors of reality. They provide an external referent for anchoring selves. Hence, institutional behaviours mobilise and shape parts and levels of individuals' selves. And, obviously, the kind of politics pursued by institutions conditions identities.

Probably, most theorists think implicitly of collaborative politics as the referent to construct the notion of multilevel identities. In response to this view, opinion polls in plurinational states such as Spain give a significant amount of answers of these persons that conceived themselves as regional (national) state and European, that is persons that can perceive referents for identity at several institutional levels. But it is equally logical that if politics become confrontational, this unavoidably projects a similar confrontation between levels of identity. Institutions may compete for individuals' allegiance and this does not necessarily resolve in a stable and harmonic identity in which political conflict is rationalised. The assertion of an institutional level over the remaining means probably a progressive parallel configuration of identity in which that layer becomes also the main source for identity. Finally, institutional confrontation between levels may activate paradoxically visceral identitarian dimensions that reaffirm the primacy of a primordial level.

Within the EU, there exist at least three territorial levels to be taken into account, each of them with potential capability for providing referents for identity construction. Thus, even the modest capability of the EU can affect individuals' perceptions and, from these, individuals' identities (Closa forthcoming). What interests most here is not the consideration of levels in isolation but rather their interaction. For the sake of expediency, the consideration of just the two major institutional actors (i.e. central governments and EU authorities) conveys a description of the effects on identities that can be extrapolated to a third level. Relations between these two levels of government have followed both collaborative and confrontational lines from either of which derive very different meanings for individuals. Institutional collaborative logics (lacking the EU of the kind of emotional attachment characteristic of nations) probably foster the rationalisation of the most exclusivist dimensions of self that are challenged and questioned by these collaborative dynamics. But, on the other hand, confrontational institutional logics induce a restoration of national identities that find confirmation of some of their basic tenets (such as the neighbour as the enemy and so forth). Central governments' strategies within the EU tend towards this confrontational position; national governments use to practice blame avoidance and also national institutions do occasionally fall in performative contradictions: rhetoric Europeanist discourses are contradicted by everyday behaviour in pursuit of self-interest.

The background for identity formation complicates if a third level is introduced because in this position, institutions might be tempted to forge alliances against each other in their competition for citizens' loyalty. Then, EU citizens have moving institutional constellations as referents for their identities. The manner and foundation for fitting these differ substantially. Most likely, the model of nested identities (in the sense of one encapsulated within a larger one as Russian dolls) is a meaningful image for some regions and sub-state identities. In this model, conflicts are resolved by the predominance of lower levels. But this neutralises, to some extent the possibility of EU citizenship becoming the basis for a post-national identity. Referring only to the institutional configuration (and leaving aside identity dimensions) Bader (taking part for a stronger EU citizenship) argues that multi-layered citizenship implies no foundational or hierarchical relationship between national and European citizenship in the sense that membership in lower level polities is not seen as a precondition of membership in the higher level polities, that is one could be a legal citizen of the Union without being a citizen of one of the member states (which currently is not a factual description but normative wishful thinking). In his words, this looks like a strange anomaly (Bader 1999: 171). Logically, the affirmation of supremacy of a given institutional level also means its prevalence as primary referent for identity formation. This is basically the kind of situation of the current relationship between EU citizenship and nationality of member states (Closa 1995).

In summary, models of multilevel or multilayer citizenship obviate the permanent instability and possible conflict between levels and their translation into identity formation. This pessimistic account should not however be misleading; it rather underlines the constant necessity for rationalisation processes when several levels coincide as referents for identity formation.

## Conclusion

European integration induces a redefinition of the basic form of political domination around which institutions such as citizenship have been constructed – the nation-state. Simultaneously, the EU acts as de facto empowerment for new institutional settings for individuals (EU citizenship) and minority nations within member states. At the same time, globalisation reinforces the normative strength of claims for institutional arrangements alternative to the ones provided by nation-states. However, expectations on the EU capability for acting as a *deus ex machina* and catering for the necessities of recognition of minority nations within member states should not be overemphasised. As in many other respects, the main value of the EU is the constraints, conditions and limitations for states' self-defined behaviour that occasionally may act against the legitimate rights of national minorities.

## References

Bader, V.M. (1999) 'Citizenship of the European Union: Human rights, rights of citizens and of Member States', *Ratio Juris* 12:2, 153–181.
Bauböck, R. (1997) *Citizenship and National Identities in the European Union*, Harvard Jean Monnet Working Papers no. 4, Cambridge, Mass.
Beck, U. (1999) *What is Globalisation?* London, Polity Press.

Borras-Alomar, S., T. Christiansen and A. Rodríguez-Pose (1994) 'Towards a "Europe of the Regions"? Visions and reality from a critical perspective', *Regional Politics and Policy* 4:2, 1–27.

Closa, C. (1995) 'Citizenship of the Union and nationality of Member States', *Common Market Law Journal* 32, 487–518.

Closa, C. (1997) 'Supranational citizenship and democracy: normative and empirical dimensions', in M. La Torre (ed.) *European Citizenship: An Institutional Challenge*, The Hague, Martinus Nijhoff.

Closa, C. (forthcoming) 'Between EU constitution and individuals' self: European citizenship', *Law and Philosophy*.

Decaux, E. (1998) 'Les nouveaux cadres du droit des minorités nationales en Europe', in R. Kastoryano (ed.) *Quelle identité pour l'Europe? Le multiculturalisme à l'épreuve*, Paris, Presses de Sciences Po.

Douglas, M. (1986) *How Institutions Think*, Syracuse, NY, Syracuse University Press.

Ferrajoli, L. (1993) 'Cittadinanza e diritti fondamentali', *Teoría Política* 9:3, 63–76.

Ferrajoli, L. (1999) *Derechos y garantías: La ley del más débil*, Madrid, Trotta.

Goetz, K.H. (1995) 'National governance and European integration: intergovernmental relations in Germany', *Journal of Common Market Studies* 33:1, 91–115.

Jáuregui, G. (1997) *Los nacionalismos minoritarios y la Unión Europea*, Barcelona, Ariel.

Keating, M. (1996) *Nations Against the State*, London, Macmillan.

Kymlicka, W. and W. Norman (1994) 'The return of the citizen: a survey of recent work on citizenship theory', *Ethics* 104:2, 352–381.

Lyons, C. (1996) 'Citizenship in the Constitution of the European Union: rhetoric or reality?', in R. Bellamy and D. Castiglione (eds) *Constitutionalism, Democracy and Sovereignty*, Aldershot, Avebury.

Marks, G. and I. Llamazares (1995) 'La transformación de la movilización regional en la Unión Europea' *Revista de Estudios Políticos* 22:1, 149–170.

Meehan, E. (1993) *Citizenship and the European Community*, London, Sage.

Morata, F. (1996) 'Spain', in R. Rometsch and W. Wessels (eds) *The European Union and its Member States*, Manchester, Manchester University Press.

Requejo, F. (1998) 'European citizenship in plurinational states: Some limits to traditional democratic theories: *Rawls* and *Habermas*', in U.K. Preuss and F. Requejo (eds) *European Citizenship, Multiculturalism and the State*, Baden-Baden, Nomos.

Shaw, J. (1997) 'European Union Citizenship: the IGC and beyond', *European Public Law* 3:3, 413–439.

Soysal, Y. (1994) *Limits of Citizenship: Migrants and Postnational Membership in Europe*, Chicago, University of Chicago Press.

Soysal, Y. (1996) 'Changing boundaries of civic participation: organized Islam in European public spheres', Manuscript, European University Institute, Florence.

Toggenburg, G. (2000) 'A rough orientation through a delicate relationship: the European Union's endeavours for (its) minorities', *European Integration online Papers* 4:16 http://eiop.or.at

# 7 The limits of a multinational Europe

## Democracy and immigration in the European Union

*Ricard Zapata*

## Introduction

Current debates on European citizenship are based on two premises, which broadly follow an EU-based logic and a state-based logic: on the one hand, EU citizenship represents a good; on the other, a burden. A good, in contrast to a burden, always supposes a benefit rather than a loss. From the perspective of an EU-based logic, EU citizenship constitutes a good, because it supposes freedom of movement and security to nationals of the member states. According to a state-based logic however, EU citizenship is viewed as a burden, since it entails a loss of sovereignty and the basis of its traditional political legitimacy. However, there is a third perspective, held by resident immigrants in member states, namely that the whole issue is discussed behind their backs and is one in which they have no say.

In this chapter, I will try to break the interdependence of the first two logical propositions with the help of arguments constructed from the third perspective. I will address the question of whether it is still defensible from a multinational perspective for the European Union to legitimise its admission policies and grant rights in keeping with a state-based logic and its principle of discrimination against foreigners on the basis of nationality. Normatively, the argument I wish to explore is that a European immigration policy which did not use foreigners' nationality as a guiding criterion would be more democratic. From an institutional stance, I will defend a replacement of nationality by residence as the basis for granting European citizenship. In practice, this would mean that the EU would have to change its current institutional policies towards immigrants, rethink the basis of the political legitimacy of democracy in multinational contexts, and discard its current state-based logic.

To embark on this line of reasoning, one first has to come to grips with the link between democracy and nationality. From this basis, I will examine whether the issue of foreigners' nationality, still used as the main guiding criterion for admission and accommodation procedures by the state, can be divorced from the notion of an immigration policy at EU level. The analytical advantage of this focus is that it permits separate treatment of immigration policy and state-nationality – two issues, which tend to be confused. However, I am not claiming that removing nationality issues from immigration policies would automatically render the latter more democratic. Clearly, there are other matters which have to be taken into account. Even at state level, issues concerning the relationship of these two areas are far from straightforward (Schwartz 1995). I shall examine just one aspect of this complexity and consider the potential for further exploration of this line of research.

The first section has two closely inter-connected subsections. In the first of these, I will review the arguments of Walzer, one of the first scholars to introduce the language of democracy to the phenomenon of immigration. In the second, I will set out from the basis of Walzer's appeal to construct a theory of democracy taking immigration as its starting point, and use this to frame some of the issues arising from the current debate at state level. In the second section, I will suggest what I consider to be non-negotiable basic requirements in constructing an evaluation benchmark. My main argument will be that basic democratic principles can be restated in terms of non-discrimination against foreigners on the basis of their national origin. At this stage, I will argue that this principle plays pivotal but different roles when applied at the access and coexistence levels because it depends on inclusive and public foundations respectively. In the third section, I will briefly examine three normative model options where I consider the practical impact of these requirements: the assimilationist, the integrationist, and the autonomous models. These three models establish different versions of political legitimacy in the public sphere of multicultural democracies. In the fourth section, I will argue for an abandonment of considerations of foreigners' nationality at an institutional level when applying these ideas to the European Union. After a brief historical overview of the institutions, the need to establish a category of *Euro-foreigner* without assumptions of nationality will be justified, questioning normatively the current institutional dysfunctions of a potentially multinational Europe. This could serve as one of the prerequisites for a future multinational Europe, whose immigration policy would be detached from traditional state-based logic. It would then be possible to bring the

European political process into line with the multinational context – a more realistic stance which is also a great deal more legitimate from a democratic standpoint.

## The language of democracy applied to immigration: some issues in the current debate

I consider Michael Walzer as one of the first scholars to detect the practical problems posed by liberalism's conceptual capital when trying to place immigration issues within the framework of a theory of democracy. He leaves us the task of examining some aspects of liberal theory in order to re-orient its practice. Foreshadowing some of the arguments defended today in the work of Kymlicka (1989, 1995), the main practical problem of liberal theory is that it assumed cultural homogeneity in the political communities under theoretical consideration.[1] This liberal assumption raises the issue of the implicit relationship between state-nationality (citizenship) and politics, and leads to discussion of the need to separate them, similar to the discussion concerning religion in the past.

Historically, state-nationality either stemmed from political considerations, or political decisions were taken on the basis of state-nationality. A plural cultural context (the result of immigration) renders this historical relationship outdated. In other words, acquisition of citizenship, understood as a political process of embracing social diversity, did not necessarily imply cultural assimilation (Walzer 1982: 12). This line of thought thus expresses an explicit rejection of ethnic policies which amount to institutional racism (Dummet and Nicol 1990; Kellas 1991; Wieviorka 1997, 1998).

Walzer proposes several ways in which institutions can recognise the multicultural basis of the societies they serve. These include: state defence of collective rights; a policy of celebrating non-state cultural identities; providing ethnic communities with funds for bilingual and bicultural education and group-oriented welfare services; and a right to some sort of representation in state agencies with responsibilities in these spheres (1982: 19–21). The state, faced with the problem of cultural pluralism, can intervene in two basic ways to restructure group life: it can apply an *autonomist* or an *integrationist strategy*. In the first case, the state can encourage groups to organise themselves, assigning them a political role in the state apparatus, institutionalising cultural differences. In the second case, the state acts to reduce differences among groups by establishing symmetrical achievement standards for their members. This latter option, if applied generally, tends to repress every sort of cultural specificity, turning ethnic identity into an administrative classification, regulated by the principle of loyalty to state institutions (Walzer 1982: 24, 27).

These arguments show the need to reconsider cultural difference as an autonomous collective good to be incorporated in the list of liberal primary goods. However, they also reveal how the practical problems of cultural pluralism challenge liberal theory to seriously reconsider traditional institutional structures. This problem receives special treatment in one of the first chapters of Walzer's *Spheres of Justice* (1983, henceforth *SJ*). The initial argument could be formulated as follows: when we think of democracy, we think of independent states capable of arranging their own patterns of division and exchange. We assume the existence of an established group and a fixed population and so we miss the first and most important distributive question: how is that group constituted (*SJ*, 31)? Nowadays, the issue which cultural pluralism poses for liberal theory is whether it is democratic for nation-states to run their economies with the help of people excluded from holding citizenship (*SJ*, 55). Put another way, can one justify states depriving people of the right to make life choices simply on the basis of their nationality (*SJ*, 54)? The conventional nature of citizenship (without natural or religious foundations of legitimisation) implies that it is a primary good regulated in the same way as any other state-distributed good, through determinate criteria. In this respect it is difficult not to agree with Walzer, that *the criteria of admission that liberal tradition uses are far from being unquestionable.* A look at his arguments will be helpful at this juncture.

In all liberal states the process of admission is twofold: the first stage covers admission of immigrants while the second concerns naturalisation (*SJ*, 42–51). Two types of admission criteria are employed at the first stage. These two criteria can be qualitative or quantitative, specifying either the type of person or the number of people who may be admitted, respectively.[2]

From a qualitative point of view, the conditions for admission mirror the character of the host community. This is why one of the first conditions for permitting access to a country is regulated by the *principle of recognition of national affinity (SJ, 42)*. One of the problems of this currently employed principle is that it is one-sided, since it is applied only to non-nationals. For nationals, non-recognition of national affinity is not a reason for expulsion. In liberal theory there is then *asymmetry* between immigration and emigration. This nationality principle thus suffers from an important limitation.

Other problems are posed if quantitative immigration criteria are adopted instead of principles of national affinity. This criterion, in contrast with the previous one, is viewed as a social good (*SJ*, 44–45). It can be considered as a measure designed to protect 'living space'. However, is a political community justified in denying the needy access merely because they are 'foreigners'? The practice of liberalism shows us that the *principle of mutual aid* has been interpreted from a utilitarian standpoint and not from the ethical standpoint theoretically upheld by some liberal theorists.[3]

Other criteria have in the past guided (and continue to guide) state treatment of foreigners. Arguments of insufficient living space and high population densities are frequently deployed to deny admission to a country and its welfare benefits. These arguments highlight the limitations of tolerance. The same applies to qualitative external criteria based on wealth and resources and regulated by utilitarian principles, that, as Walzer points out, boil down to primitive and parochial versions of the Rawlsian difference principle: immigration can be restricted as soon as failure to do so would 'interfere materially with the efforts of the government to maintain an adequately high standard of living among the members of the community generally, especially the poorest classes' (*SJ*, 48).

To sum up Walzer's arguments, the principle of democracy is this: that the process of self-determination through which a state shapes its internal life must be *equally open* to all those who live in the country, work in the local economy, and are subject to local law. When second admissions (i.e., naturalisation, which depends on first admissions – immigration) are closed, the political economy collapses into a world of members and outsiders, with no political boundaries between the two, and where the outsiders are subject to the members. No democratic state can tolerate the establishment of a fixed status difference between citizen and foreigner. A sound democratic policy has to make a choice: if it opts to admit people, it must treat them equally, without discriminating on the basis of their nationality, and, once admitted, must accept their full accommodation in the body politic. This is the responsible choice that states must make. This means doing away with foreigners' nationality as a policy guideline. One might go so far as to say that this structural problem of liberalism is what makes it work since the system would soon fail without denial of political rights and the ever-present threat of deportation. This kind of tacit liberal consensus is not legitimated by any theory of democracy (*SJ*, 58).[4]

Hence the appeal to construct a theory of democracy taking immigration as its starting point. Efforts have been made in this direction during the 1990s, in the light of the need to adapt notions of citizenship to a new world order.[5]

With regard to the link between democracy and immigration, we can say that the literature of the 1990s can be considered under two headings: nationality and economics. Each of these heading lies at the root of our definition of 'foreignness' and hence foreigners. One covers the notion of the foreigner as a vehicle for cultural values at odds with the host nationality; the other, foreigners as a commodity for the host community. Even though the issues under each heading are quite different, both force states to define their responsibilities and to modify their basic institutional structure for admitting and accommodating immigrants.

The *heading of nationality* (used in the sense of culture, in a broad sense, including race, ethnicity, religion, national origin and even language)[6] is perhaps the most difficult one. These assumptions have to do with what Elster (1989) calls the cement of society. The main question is about the connection between nationality and immigration. May a state decide not to admit immigrants for the sake of preserving existing national patterns? If a state decides to admit immigrants, may it take nationality into account in the selection process? Liberal states are, by definition, committed to individual freedom and autonomy, and thus to the pluralism that follows from the right of individuals to pursue their own conceptions of right and wrong. Unfortunately, liberalism simply has no conceptual tools to formulate coherent answers when whole groups adopt differing value systems. In a strong liberal state, borders should be open to all since there are no liberal principles that legitimise limitations to access (Carens 1987, 1997; Schwartz 1995; Bader 1997). Even if limits can be justified, once immigrants live in a country, there are no liberal justifications for limiting public identity and action to a part of the population. Such justification is even more difficult in the context of globalisation. Two facts must be borne in mind here: first, personal freedom of movement is much more limited than that enjoyed by services, goods, and capital; second, the current status of foreigners is similar to the situation prevailing throughout the nineteenth century (and much of the twentieth), when most of the national population was denied the right to vote on the basis of property ownership or gender (Balibar 1992; de Lucas 1994; Schnapper 1994), something which contrasts starkly with modern Human Rights concerns. From this point of view, the legitimising criterion today is not property or sex, but nationality. One can reasonably ask whether the relationship between nationality and democracy can still work at this level (Waldron 1992; Miller 1995; Oomen 1997; Held 1997; Zolo 1997), and whether these two historically linked notions are now compatible from the standpoint of an immigration policy. It seems something has to give: immigration policies based mainly on nationality criteria run counter to the spirit and political realities of this new global age. Here I am interested to show that these problems of matching theory and practice could at least be partially solved, if we were to dispense with the principle of national affinity in legitimising the practice of liberal states towards foreigners, both at the level of access and coexistence.

The *second heading* raises similar issues at different levels. The principle guiding liberal state practices is not greater national or cultural diversity, but the market in general and the national labour market in particular. However, the same discriminatory effects result. In theory, liberalism has defended the freedom of movement of individuals as well as capital (Barry and Goodin 1992; Hollifield 1992). In practice, the admission criteria for immigrants and subsequent accommodation raise problems of democracy because economic considerations come into play. The common assumption is that states are entitled to adopt whatever immigration policies they judge to be in their economic interest. From this viewpoint, states are free to limit access if immigration increases unemployment or the welfare tax burden. In contrast, the doors are thrown open if immigration proves to be economically advantageous (one only has to recall the 'guest-worker' programmes, for instance). Here, that immigrants are viewed as a commodity is evident. Thus even when the basis for admission is economic rather than of nationality, the same problems arise.[7] Is it democratically legitimate to select immigrants on the basis of what they can contribute economically (Carens 1995: 6–9)? Is it democratically acceptable to let employers lobby governments in choosing which immigrants are most likely to make a productive contribution? Is the quota policy favoured by liberal states to regulate immigration democratically defensible?

As this brief introduction of issues reveals, the language of democracy in connection with immigration is anything but straightforward. The link between democracy, nationality and foreigners ultimately mirrors some of the most fundamental questions of the limits of state policy. To what extent is it legitimate for liberal states to pursue national (and economic) interests, and to what extent ought they concern themselves with the interests of foreigners? Is it a question of 'anything goes' or are there democratic bounds to liberal state practices? If so, where do these limits lie? Once we have mapped them, how do we give them institutional expression? My contribution here is to introduce this discourse and to venture some answers addressing these questions in a plurinational polity: the European Union.

## Democracy and foreigners: basic non-negotiable requirements for a critical standard for evaluation

To embark on an analysis of the relationship between democracy and foreigners we must first delimit the meaning of each.

By 'foreigners' I understand a state-dependent concept, that is the conditions and norms which regulate their activities stem from the sovereignty of the state, which is the only active component in a vertical relationship.[8] In terms of rights, foreigners may be granted social, economic and civil rights but, by definition, are not permitted to participate in public life. From an analytical point of view, while 'citizenship' is a fixed notion which describes a stable situation, 'foreigner' is by nature a dynamic term describing an unstable and transitory condition. I should now like to fix the other component of the relationship, namely, 'democracy'.

When I speak of democracy, the language I use is the language of final moral judgement. Democracy establishes the legitimate parameters of public policy (Carens 1995: 10). In the main literature on this issue, this component is based on the principle of equality. In this context, this basically means the principle of non-discrimination against foreigners on the basis of their national origin. My contention is that this principle plays a pivotal but different role when applied at the admission and coexistence stages, because it depends on two corresponding foundations: inclusion and the right to play a role in public life respectively. I will suggest that rigorous application of this principle at both levels requires that national origin be dropped as a criterion of immigration policy.

### *The principle of equality when applied at the access level and its inclusive foundation*

In placing the status of foreigners within the context of a wider reflection on democracy, we are faced with a decision between who is included in the territorial unit and who is excluded (Walzer 1993: 55). Inclusion thus seems to be one of the distinguishing foundations of the equality principle when applied to access.

Exclusion, in turn, can function in two ways. It can be applied to all foreigners regardless of their national origin, or can depend on variables such as language, culture, historical and geographical affinities and so on. In other words, exclusion may be universal or selective: it can either discriminate between citizens and foreigners (whatever their national origin) or among all foreigners (taking their national origin as criterion).

The key issue with regard to this foundation is the decision regarding who belongs to the *territorial* unit and who does not. It also gives rise to a second related problem which goes to the heart of the matter: namely, that the decision is based on national identity. Traditionally, in Europe at least, it has been taken for granted that the *territory* and the *nation* coincide (Hobsbawm 1990). If the whole population of a territory were 'nationals', then the problem of inclusion would not arise. I would argue that these issues share a common concern with regard to democracy: *how to reach an inclusive democracy without threatening national state identity* (Layton-Henry 1990b: 1, 22–3). This question makes sense when we apply the equality principle at the level of coexistence, once foreigners have been admitted.

## The principle of equality when applied at the coexistence level and its public foundation

At this second level, I shall discuss the reasons invoked by the state for legitimising restrictions of the equality principle for a significant part of the resident population. Taking this problem as a starting point, we find at least two opposed theoretical positions: one that invokes cosmopolitan reasons for eliminating these restrictions, and another that defends them on grounds of 'realism'. To distinguish between them, we can ask which interest is more democratically legitimate. Realists would answer the nation-state's interests, those of the cosmopolitan persuasion would say foreigners' interests. Let us briefly examine their respective arguments.[9]

The *realists* argue that democracy presupposes the determination of *demos*, and not the other way round. The specific character of the *demos* is naturally exclusive (Hailbronner 1989: 76). According to this line of reasoning, seeing the relationship between democracy and foreigners as *a problem* is simply to put the cart before the horse. They therefore consider the problem to be based on false premises. Nowadays, resident foreigners without citizenship (*denizens*: Hammar 1989) possess almost all citizen's rights outside the political sphere. In these circumstances, it is reasonable for citizens to retain for themselves the few privileges which have no economic, social and, even, psychological impact on foreigners living in a strange land (Hailbronner 1989: 79).

This frontal attack against those who implicitly present their arguments as if they were a panacea is well directed. However, there is also evidence that some basic principles of democracy are threatened when adults fully capable of acting in the public sphere are subject to a political authority that prevents them from fully expressing their culture. This is the point of departure for those in the opposing camp.

The basis of the *cosmopolitan* argument is that all resident aliens have the right to publicly express their cultural values. A state which restricts this right is acting against a basic principle of democracy: equality for all (Carens 1989: 36–37). The justification for this position is that a democratic immigration policy must permit every long-term non-national resident to exercise the moral right to participate in the public sphere, since political authority must be based solely on the consent of its population. Permanent resident aliens belong to this population, consequently their rights to act in the public sphere must be ensured.

As I proposed above, this application of the principle of equality has a *public foundation*. This foundation could be read in two ways: on the one hand, it stresses the context where the relationship between the *demos* and the state takes place. The *demos* can express its identity in the public sphere. On the other hand, it also highlights the difficulty of delimiting what any democratic theory needs to establish: the *public good*. Let us examine each reading separately.

The problem the first reading poses is that even though the activity of citizens is functionally determinant as an instrument of inclusion, it is also implicitly exclusive for those groups which cannot express their distinguishing traits in a publicly recognised form (Young 1989, 1990). Public activity thus entails cultural assimilation (in the sense of *sameness* or *likeness*), or cultural uniformity (Parekh 1991) and therefore excludes differences which are what really concern individuals. This is why the public sphere, as the distinctive sphere of citizens' activity, is considered homogeneous. The problem therefore lies in determining conditions that make it possible to establish communication between the *demos* and the state if only one part of the person is represented, namely, the part matching the identity represented within the public sphere. In this respect, recent literature poses the problem in terms of the relationship between the universality and homogeneity which supposedly applies to citizenship and the public sphere on the one hand, and the cultural or identity differences that remain within the private sphere on the other. The political question that an immigration policy has to answer is thus: *how should one manage differences within a sphere that has always tended to reduce them and treat them as politically irrelevant?*

The second reading of the public foundation starts from the premise that the *public good* and the *national good* are one and the same. This is not new. Traditionally, the public good has been considered as the exclusive good of the *demos*, not the *population*. Here the public foundation reveals another facet. While the first reading was approached in terms of access to the public sphere, this second reading deals with the exclusive goods conferred by citizenship.

This sense of 'public good' implies that an immigration policy must manage the interests of aliens and justify why they are not treated as well as normal citizens. The realists argue the need for this double standard on the basis that the interests of foreigners simply do not represent the public good. Moreover, catering to the interests of foreigners is not politically cost-effective from an electoral point of view (M. J. Miller 1989; Layton-Henry 1990b, 1990c; Andersen 1990; Rath 1990). The cosmopolitans consider that resident aliens, once their status is regularised, should benefit from most of the public goods accorded to citizens, such as education, health services, and almost all universal welfare services, but they cannot participate in determining the distribution of these goods. This reading stresses the fact that the public good does not mean the good of the whole population (as has traditionally been supposed), but only the public good of the *demos* (Dahl 1992: 354).

## Democracy and cultural pluralism within state frontiers

Today, the language of democracy sketched in the previous sections needs to be practically applied to the cultural pluralism that exists within state frontiers. This scenario can be viewed as producing strains which go to the heart of the reorientation process taking place in the liberal democratic tradition (Zapata 1999, 2000a).

The analysis in this section takes this process on board. My argument is based on the premise that liberal democracy will only triumph if it can show itself institutionally capable of managing these new tensions in a flexible fashion. This scenario often runs into serious difficulties in applying a coherent language of democracy when faced with the empirical evidence of the increasing movement of people beyond state borders (Goodin 1992; Weiner 1995, 1996; Carens 1996; Jacobson 1996).

Let me first say that when I use the term 'cultural pluralism' I mean the problems confronted by Western societies in political management of territorially dispersed immigrant groups who reside in a country for welfare and economic reasons. In this context, at least three positions have been tried historically to tackle the tensions between group customs and standard practices in the host country, while combining unity and diversity in terms of democracy (Rex 1996; Bauböck *et al.* 1996; Parekh 1998). These models of multicultural democracy (or accommodation of immigrants into host societies) can be analysed in terms of historical processes. Thus each accommodation model could be seen as expressing a historical phase mirroring state treatment of foreigners at the time.

We can sketch the guidelines adopted by each of these positions by using two key indicators. These are participation in political decision making and management of cultural differences, and the institutionally recognised culture of the public sphere. These respectively cover claims for assimilation, integration, and autonomy. I shall now examine the foundations which legitimise state treatment of foreigners.[10]

The *assimilationist model* has historically been the first reaction of a state trying to manage increasing cultural diversity produced by the presence of foreigners. This model considers any change in the cultural contents and limits enshrined in the public sphere unnecessary, despite the fact that these contents arise from a monocultural origin. Evidently, this model does not foster foreigners' participation in political management of cultural differences, an area which remains the exclusive preserve of citizens. Cultural diversity is seen from a competitive point of view, thus a culture which disposes of greater resources will be able to marshal more support within the public sphere. In terms of the two indicators, assimilation could be defined as handing policy decisions regarding cultural differences over to citizens acting within a culturally homogeneous public sphere. Consequently, foreigners who want to gain access to this public sphere will have to relegate cultural practices likely to produce tensions to the private sphere and embrace those which have already been institutionalised and publicly recognised. This model of accommodation only calls for state intervention when the native culture is seen to be threatened by those considered to be 'cultural invaders'.

The *integrationist model* is the one which currently commands most support. It is most characteristic of Western liberal democracies and represents a second stage in the state's treatment of foreigners, which occurs once it is realised immigrants have abandoned any idea of returning to their homeland and have decided to build a life in their countries of residence. Like the previous model, it defends the idea that policy for managing cultural differences should be in the hands of citizens, but accepts the need to vary some contents and cultural limits enshrined in the public sphere so as to permit recognition of some foreign cultural practices. This institutional recognition takes place so as to limit cultural conflict and ensure social stability. Advocates of this position can argue that the public sphere is pluricultural, even though decisions regarding its contents and limits are still the exclusive preserve of citizens. Those foreigners who manage to meet the criteria for acceptance applied by citizens will find it easier to press their claims. Nevertheless, citizens still have the last word on whether foreigners' cultural needs are met. In contrast with the assimilationist model, the integrationist model would reject cultural assimilation and requires foreigners to *integrate* into their host countries. This means that citizens are willing to change certain traditions in the public sphere, to 'interculturalise', but reject any political say for foreigners in managing the process.

The *autonomous model* goes a step further. Only five European countries (Sweden, 1975; Switzerland, 1975; Denmark, 1977; Norway, 1978; and The Netherlands, 1985) have entered this third phase, albeit at the local level (Lapeyronnie 1992). In common with the integrationist model, it accepts the need to create a public sphere which is sensitive to foreigners' cultural practices. It therefore supports state-led initiatives in integrating foreigners, but in contrast with both previous models, immigrants play a part in determining the policies which affect them. Its participatory nature therefore lends itself to political autonomy for foreigners. Put another way, foreigners can take part in political processes which determine the nature of the cultural contents and limits of the public sphere just like any other citizen.

Whatever positions a state adopts, all states share a common concern to find political means to secure peaceful coexistence between foreigners and citizens. Let us now pursue this line of reasoning in relation to the European Union. In passing, it must be said that the EU poses a serious challenge for political theorists interested in a theory of democracy which takes immigration into account.

## The limits of a multinational Europe

Given the main topic of this book, my aim is to emphasise that the traditional, strong historical tie between nationality and citizenship is at the core of the normative difficulties concerning the link between multinational democracy and citizenship.

From my theoretical analysis, we could draw the following rule of thumb: we need to rule out all selective exclusion and discrimination (i.e., not to differentiate among foreign nationalities) and to ensure equality of treatment and of opportunities. On the basis of this rule, we can now go on to consider European Union level, where some important recommendations can be made based on my central thesis. I will perform this task in two stages: in a first subsection, I will briefly review the history of European institutional structure; in a second subsection, I will turn to the normative challenges encountered in the European political process. My argument will be that establishing a category of *Euro-foreigner*, grounded on the basis of residence instead of the traditional state logic of nationality could provide a partial solution to these normative problems. This basis is much more legitimate if Europe wishes to preserve (and link) its multinational character and democracy.

## Brief historical review of European immigration policies[11]

In approaching EU evolution in connection with immigration, we can highlight four main stages: the beginning of intergovernmental co-operation (1975–86); Single European Act (1986–92); Maastricht Treaty and Schengen Agreement (1992–7); and Amsterdam Treaty (1998 to date).

### Beginning of intergovernmental cooperation (1975–86)

Co-operation between member states in the area of immigration increased progressively after 1975. For instance, the so-called Trevi Group was established, composed at that time of nine Home Office ministers with the aim of coordinating judicial and policing measures to combat terrorism. European institutions, however, played no role at this stage since all contacts were strictly inter-governmental. Hence, the state logic prevailed over any EU logic.

### The Single European Act (1986–92)

The Single European Act represented an important advance in the area of cooperation; however there was little transparency involved, even among European institutions. Article 8 of the Act provided institutional recognition for the first time of the freedom of movement of citizens, albeit as one of the main prerequisites to the Common Market. This freedom of movement was even included as a community matter in its own right. The working parties created on that occasion included representatives of the European Commission acting as observers. These working parties included, among others, the 'ad hoc' Group on immigration in 1986, made up of ministers with responsibilities in the area. The issue became the responsibility of the European Commission, which established Secretariats for this purpose. The European Council at the time was designed to consider judicial, penal and civil cooperation issues.

It was in that context that the Council took the first steps to link the issues of freedom of movement and security. In 1989, for instance, it recommended that the Group propose measures in this area. As a result, a working programme was drawn up, the Palma Document, which endorsed (among other measures) a more coordinated approach to justice and home affairs. The method implemented continued to be inter-governmental, that is, limited to drafting agreements, the formulation of resolutions, conclusions and recommendations – in a nutshell, all the classic resorts of International Law.

As a result of this process, two important Agreements were reached in 1990: the Dublin Agreement, and the executive Schengen Agreement. The first settled which State was responsible for examining demands for asylum in an EU member country; the second was rooted in the Schengen Agreement of 1985 and fostered the creation of new operational structures to guarantee policing and cooperation in the EU. The second agreement effectively created what might be called *Schengenland*, i.e., a progressive abolition of 'internal' border controls among the signatory states.

## The Maastricht Treaty and Schengen Agreement (1992–7)

The European Union Treaty (the 1992 EU Treaty or simply the Maastricht Treaty) represented a quantum leap in the development of the European Community. Among its distinguishing traits as far as immigration was concerned, two 'motors for change' covering every aspect of the EU constitution were created. These were the Euro in the economic field, and EU citizenship in the political. Another decisive step was the design of the three pillars on which the new EU structure was to rest. The Community – the first pillar – introduced, among other things, the concept of progressive loss of sovereignty of member states, an issue on which all three basic EU institutions – Commission, Council and Parliament – work together. In contrast, the second and third pillars continue to follow cooperation logic (state logic) and not one of integration (EU logic). The majority of decisions require unanimity and as a result the jurisdiction of states is preserved through the Council, which is where decisions are made. The second pillar (Foreign Policy and Common Security) deals with EU foreign policy, while the third pillar (Co-operation in Justice and Home Affairs) covers policies within EU borders. Thus, Maastricht provided institutional recognition for the cooperation measures introduced from 1975 onwards.

Before explaining the importance of the Schengen Agreement within this new Maastricht framework, it must be noted that the immigration issue during this period was a nettle which no one was willing to grasp. As a result, the question remained one which was more subject to state logic than to a strict EU logic. The norms contained in Section 6 (covering Cooperation in Justice and Home Affairs) are in fact more akin to the traditional norms of International Law than strictly Community Law. They limit the framework within which cooperation among states can take place. In practice, this third pillar has become notorious for the miserably limited scope it provides for making political decisions. This paralysis lies behind immigrant feeling on the issue. Its structure only gave Community institutions a partial say but denied them any real control over member states' decisions. Masterful inactivity typified the Council's work in this field since it proved impossible to obtain the unanimity needed to reach a decision. The EU perception of immigrants is clear in Article K1, which established 'common interest' fields. Immigration (access, circulation, stay, residence and work irregularities) is included in a long list along with asylum policies, norms on crossing borders, international fraud, drug trafficking, and matters of judicial, penal and civil cooperation (including terrorism, among other issues).

This institutional stereotype of the immigrant as a potential delinquent also appears in the Schengen Agreement. Its basic objective is linked to an early realisation that gradual dismantling of internal borders was needed in order to ensure real freedom of movement within the EU.[12]

In strict terms, through Schengenland the EU gave states the opportunity to use the EU institutional framework for cooperation on specific home issues. The Amsterdam Treaty will take this one step further by explicitly incorporating the Schengen provisions within the EU framework. Significantly, the post of Council Secretary General has been created. The Amsterdam Treaty seals Schengen as a set of common measures on immigration (and asylum), policing of the EU's external borders and control of so-called 'illegal' immigration. Thus, the

Amsterdam Treaty effectively gives institutional weight to a narrow juridical perception of immigration as a source of delinquency, organised crime, or just as a straightforward 'threat' to EU stability.

Since Maastricht, the non-discrimination principle as a criterion for the freedom of movement of people is only effective at the internal level of the EU and affects only citizens of the Community's member states. It does not apply to those who wish to enter the EU through its external borders, regardless of their nationality. Avoiding rhetorical arguments, it is clear that institutionally immigrants are not considered as persons, since the freedom of internal movement only benefits persons as citizens of one of the member states. How else can one explain the apparent liberalism behind the member states' agreement to internal migration on the one hand, and strict inter-governmental exclusion of immigration from outside the EU on the other? The recent Amsterdam Treaty provides some insights on this issue.

## *The Amsterdam Treaty (1998 to date)*

The Amsterdam Treaty came about as the result of the negotiations in Maastricht where agreement was reached to hold an Intergovernmental Conference in the second half of the 1990s with a view to completely revising the EU Treaty (Edwards and Wiessala 1998). In my view, the new structure arising from Amsterdam introduces at least three broad changes: reform of the common policy on immigration and asylum *vis-à-vis* third country nationals (erroneously termed the 'communitarisation' of the third pillar); the incorporation of a new objective: an area of freedom, justice and security; the integration of the so-called Schengen absorption clause (the provisions on visas, borders and procedures negotiated under the Schengen Agreement would now automatically be incorporated into the EU treaty); and confirmation of EU citizenship. All these 'changes' simply reveal the conservatism of the EU on immigration matters, which often falls little short of hypocrisy. Before overviewing these changes separately, I should perhaps justify this statement.

Even given the complex interaction between issues of freedom, security and justice, one cannot help but be surprised by the absence of basic principles of equality and pluralism in the EU's new objectives (set out in Article B). The only reference to pluralism appears not in connection with culture or stateless nations but with the media (*Protocol on the public system of media of the member states*). The word equality appears only in relation to equality of opportunities and sex discrimination (new Articles 2 and 3, Articles 118 and 119).

In this case, there is no mention of equality between citizens and immigrants. The term *foreigner* is not mentioned and the words *immigrant* and *immigration* are only included as measures to cover issues of freedom, security and justice. Immigration is implicitly viewed as something which threatens freedom and is an area in which the legislators have succumbed to fear, protectionism and concerns over border control. In this sense, the modifications to the Treaty, instead of expressing a qualitative change, explicitly manifest a desire for continuity. Once again, immigration has been pigeon-holed along with security and control issues, for which new legal instruments have been dreamt up. Let me now examine some aspects of these three reforms.

## Communitarisation of the third pillar

One of the 'great reforms' of the Amsterdam Treaty is to have shifted some of the issues that previously were treated in the third pillar into the first pillar, that is, into the EU's normal policy-making institutions. Communitarisation extends not only to visa, asylum and immigration policy but also to judicial cooperation in civil matters with cross-border implications. Police cooperation and criminal matters remain in the inter-governmental third pillar, now called *Cooperation in policing and judicial matters in penal affairs*. But this Communitarisation will still be subject to state logic until 2006 until the requirement for unanimous decisions is waived. In this respect, to speak of reform seems premature to say the least. The gain is a very modest one – majority voting in 2006, assuming unanimity can be summoned for its implementation.

## New objective: an area of freedom, justice and security

'Communitarisation' is grounded on the explicit connection between the freedom of movement of persons (i.e. EU citizens), and the need to adopt measures to guarantee the safety of people within this area (Valle 1998). It is not only the establishment of this link which is new but also the way it has been institutionalised through Common Law. One needs only look at the plans laid at the Cardiff meeting (December 1998) to see the way issues of freedom, security and justice were framed.

Even the most superficial reading of the Cardiff papers is enough to reveal the negative application of notions of freedom regarding movement, living according to the law, protection of human rights and respect for individual privacy. Accordingly, security is mainly related to guaranteeing an individual's rights in the private sphere and justice to a Community-based concept of Common Law held by its citizens.

The EU logic is, we can say, of the first order: allowing freedom of movement across member states' borders could endanger the security of EU citizens. Freedom implies security. Crimes and offences can transcend state borders and, indeed, exploit them (the list is endless: terrorism, delinquency, drug trafficking, fraud, even racism and xenophobia). This is why the EU must have the juridical instruments (justice) to protect its citizens from these foreign perils (hence the obsession with security).

Immigration is directly affected by this closed logic, since European politicians perceive it as just another threat. In this sense, the Amsterdam Treaty recommends specific measures to create a common policy of controls and admission covering its external borders. The following measures are contemplated at the internal level over the next five years: the total suppression of border control of persons, both EU citizens and EU foreigners; at the external level, a long list of common control norms and procedures, including a uniform model visa for third-country nationals and for nationals exempt from visa requirements; admission and residence conditions; common norms on granting permanent residence permits; norms to fight against clandestine immigration and irregular residence; norms on expulsion; common rights of regular immigrants; and the conditions attached to their movement among member states.

## European citizenship

The Maastricht Treaty gave the notion of EU citizenship institutional recognition. This new political concept continues to play a pivotal role within the political framework of the EU. It is confined to an extension of electoral rights – to vote in and stand for local and European elections – for nationals of the member states residing in an EU country other than their own, a confirmation of the existing right to petition the European Parliament, the establishment of an ombudsman and sharing of consular services outside the EU. Despite the heated political debate that the Maastricht Treaty gives rise to, there is a common conviction that its importance is more symbolic than real. But the fact that it dodged any commitment on the issue of a single EU nationality, gave rise to a wide-ranging debate on whether this new political category complements or rivals the common sovereignty of states (Cesarini and Fulbrook 1996; Lehning and Weale 1997).

Aware of these controversies, the Amsterdam Treaty completes Article 8 of Maastricht by confirming that citizenship of the Union *will complement but not replace* that of member states. The nature of EU citizenship has thus been definitively established.

## Normative challenges: questionable institutional dysfunctions in a multinational Europe

The asymmetrical nature of economic and political integration in the European Union lies at the heart of the problem of the limits of a multinational Europe. In this chapter, I have used the immigration issue to show where these limits are most apparent. Economic and political integration are proceeding at different rates and are driven by different forces: this can be seen clearly in the case of the Euro and the citizenship issue, respectively. On the political level, the language of democracy is still on the wish list. The economic process has had a long head start over the political one, which at the time of writing is only nine years old and hence commands weaker institutional support at the political level. The link between both has not yet been established.

We can highlight at least six interconnected issues for normative consideration. In keeping with my argument, all of these indicate that the EU logic must prevail if the new Europe is to come to terms with the multinational make-up of its societies. This means opposing the state-inspired logic which has held sway to date. At present, states give some leeway to the EU in policy making but are always wary of any attempt to weaken their grasp in this field.

1   When we approach this area from the perspective of the Euro-foreigners (Zapata 1998a, 1998b), the paradox is even clearer. Euro-foreigners simply have no right to freedom of movement. They may perhaps enjoy social rights if they attain permanent resident status (as *denizens*) but, because of the lack of freedom of movement, they are deprived of such rights in other EU countries. When they move from one EU country to another, they cannot transfer the limited rights conceded by a given member state. There are just too many frontiers and barriers for foreigners in the EU. The EU simply does not exist for them and if it does, it is being built behind their backs and belongs to a 'privileged' club from which they are excluded.

2   We are again witnessing the construction of a *demos* which, instead of enlarging its limits qualitatively, is doing so quantitatively, retaining an unwavering state logic. This only becomes apparent

when we approach the matter from the standpoint of the frequently debated European public identity. This public identity is being constructed in opposition to 'non-European others'. This is clear when Euro-barometers describe the negative perception Euro-citizens have of Euro-foreigners (Ugur 1998: 308). This emerging evidence of a European identity invites us to at least take the normative reflection seriously. Euro-foreigners simply have no place in this emergent European public identity.

3   From the normative viewpoint of democracy proposed here, there is a pressing need to start a theoretical and institutional debate on the immigration model which the EU should adopt. As I have pointed out in the past (Zapata 1998c), if we want to speak of European citizenship in promoting a political multinational union in Europe, we ought to be able to speak of the category of Euro-foreigners – which is impossible at the moment. Similarly, if we want to speak of a political Europe, we ought to be able to speak of a single immigration policy, not fifteen. When these issues are addressed, they will need to be guided by the principles of democracy sketched out above. Without a willingness to address them, future policy will undoubtedly get mired in specious new justifications for ignoring the democratic deficit in Europe. We cannot begin a discourse on democracy unless we first face up to the asymmetrical situation experienced by foreigners in the EU.

4   This debate can take place on two levels: the case of foreigners already living in a country who wish to participate in decision-making processes which directly affect them; and the case of foreigners wishing to gain admission, which directly affects state decisions. Even if these two levels ought to draw on different principles, it is also evident that they are interconnected. The second directly affects the first. In the first case, the criterion of foreigners' nationality ought to disappear and be replaced by the criterion of residence (the principle of *residents' Europe* rather than the more popular *citizens' Europe*). Three to five years of residence ought to be enough for foreigners to be allowed to participate politically and enjoy a degree of autonomy. The principle of universal inclusion should be applied in the second case (the principle that *control based on foreigners' national origin is democratically indefensible*). This principle of universal inclusion applied at the European level would mean scrapping considerations of cultural affinity or preferences still found in some state immigration policies. To sum up: foreigners, whatever their national origins, should enjoy equal treatment and be given opportunities to enter Europe. Foreigners

already living in Europe should have a say in formulating policies. Letting foreigners participate in decision-making processes obeys the principle that *denizens should not be deprived of opportunities for political accommodation* (the autonomous model introduced above).

5 Another issue deserving normative considerations and based on the framework sketched above, is the pejorative connotation attached to foreign status in the EU, in spite of the effort to use 'politically correct' language in the recent Amsterdam Treaty. Since the Maastricht Treaty, the situation is as follows: there is a formal institutionalisation of European citizenship, which corresponds to the first pillar, and there is consequently a common policy and integration field. The antonymous notion, 'foreigner', corresponds (despite the Amsterdam Treaty) to the third pillar, and is a subject of common interest covering inter-governmental cooperation. This institutional dysfunction is one of the main practical problems and explains why it is still impossible to speak of a full European democratic citizenship, with its own distinctive content and independence from member states. Moreover, the scope contemplated by the third pillar, where common interest serves as the basis for legitimisation of restrictions on people's freedom of movement, is very clear. Foreigners are put on a par with drug-traffickers, terrorists and international criminals.

6 Finally, to initiate reflection on the topic, we must face up to the *asymmetrical situation experienced by foreigners in the EU*. At the moment, in spite of the formal existence of European citizenship, a foreigner (for instance a Latin American) wishing to enter and live in Spain enjoys a status quite unlike that he or she would be accorded in Germany. In part, this is due to the variety of traditions in European states regarding treatment of foreigners and their concepts of citizenship. The need to build a category of *Euro-foreigner* is evidently a prerequisite to any future European immigration law. Clearly, application of considerations of nationality can have no place in formulating this policy.

## Acknowledgements

Previous versions of this chapter were presented in several workshops: Centro de Teoría Política (Madrid, UAM, March 1997); *XVII IPSA World Congress* (Seoul, Korea, August 1997); *Colloquium on Philosophy and the Social Sciences, Institute of Philosophy*, Czech Academy of Sciences (Prague, May 1998); *IPSA Research Committee on Political*

*Philosophy* (Rotterdam, June 1998), and *Twenty-seventh European Consortium for Political Research* (Mannheim, March 1999). I thank all the participants for their comments. I am particularly grateful to W. Norman, F. Requejo and I. M. Young, for useful discussions and advice.

## Notes

1  In a recent work, Walzer emphasises that social cultural homogeneity has never existed. When we speak in these terms we mean that 'a single dominant group organises the common life in a way that reflects its own history and culture and, if things go as intended, carries the history forward and sustains the culture. . . . Among histories and cultures, the nation-State is not neutral; its political apparatus is an engine for national reproduction' (Walzer 1997: 25). In the last resort, this justifies the efforts of the dominant cultural group to perpetuate its own survival, regardless of others and to legislate accordingly.

2  These analytical distinctions are not Walzer's, but can be introduced in order to clarify the issues involved.

3  For Walzer, this principle has oriented admission policies since it was tacitly assumed that small numbers of immigrants would have no significant impact on the character of the political community and therefore not impinge on citizens' liberties. Ideological or ethnic affinity can be employed once the general principle of mutual aid no longer serves to legitimise admission because it produces prejudicial effects for the host society. In practice then, this theoretically non-discriminatory liberal principle of mutual aid becomes oriented by foreigners' nationality and ideology (*SJ*, 49–50).

4  It is true that Walzer gives some arguments for discriminating between foreigners at the access stage. However, he places insufficient stress on admission obligations, an observation I owe to I. M. Young. His rationale allows us to accept that these limits should be applied equally to everyone, independently of the nationality of the applicant. Despite his defence of limits on admission, Walzer's most critical arguments address what happens once foreigners have been admitted.

5  Mainly under the pressure of globalisation and multiculturalism in its two main dimensions: the plurality of national identities and immigration. See Axtmann (1996) and the other chapters of this volume and their bibliographical references.

It is not possible to cover the full complexity of this argument here. Accordingly, I will limit myself to opening up this line of research. I am, however, convinced that nationality is an artificial construct which is employed in much the same way as religion was in the past and has more to do with outmoded notions of 'loyalty' than the needs of modern states. This current system of allegiance is the core issue facing liberal democratic institutions today in accommodating immigrants. Institutions need to change as a result. The problem is what to put in nationality's place: constitutional patriotism? (Habermas 1992–3, 1999;

Nussbaum and Cohen 1996). This is not an issue I address here since my purpose is to question considerations of foreigners' nationality in any immigration policy, especially in the context of our acceptance of increasingly multicultural societies.

6 I broadly take the cultural definition of nation linked to Tamir's project (1993: 8–9).

7 I have made an attempt in Zapata (2000b).

8 It is obvious that the power of the state to determine these conditions is not unlimited, but depends on an international framework which is two-sided: on the one hand, the norms of International Law in general; on the other, the international (bilateral or multilateral) agreements and treaties ratified by the state (Robertson and Merrills 1993; Cassese 1993). These two sides of the International framework evidently have an inclusive consequence for the status of foreigners. In the following analysis, I will make a clear distinction between these 'International State duties' with regard to the state's immigration policy (Soysal 1994; Bauböck 1994).

9 A more detailed account has been made in a recent review article, including recent literature on these matters (see R. Zapata, 2000e).

10 I follow the three models sketched in a more detailed form in R. Zapata (2000d).

11 This section sums up the main arguments of R. Zapata (2000c). See also A. Geddes (2000).

12 This gradual aspect is also apparent in the process of incorporation into this new 'Schengen area', signed in June 1985 by five countries (Belgium, the Netherlands, Luxembourg, Germany and France). After the Application Agreement of June 1990 the following were incorporated into the Schengen area: Italy (November 1990), Spain and Portugal (June 1991), Greece (November 1992), Austria (April 1995) and finally Finland, Sweden and Denmark (December 1996), and (even without being EU members) Norway and Iceland. In total, Schengenland comprises 13 countries. Great Britain and Ireland continue to remain outside the Schengen accords in splendid isolation.

# References

Andersen, U. (1990) 'Consultative institutions for migrant workers', in Layton-Henry (ed.).

Axtmann, R. (1996) *Liberal Democracy into the Twenty-first Century: Globalisation, Integration and the Nation State*, Manchester: Manchester University Press.

Bader, V. (1997) 'Fairly open borders', in (ed.) *Citizenship and Exclusion*, London: Macmillan.

Balibar, E. (1992) *Les Frontières de la Démocratie*, Paris: La Découverte.

Barry, B. and Goodin, R. E. (eds) (1992) *Free Movement: Ethical Issues in the Transnational Migration of People and of Money*, University Park, Pa: Pennsylvania State University Press.

Bauböck, R. (ed.) (1994) *From Aliens to Citizens: Redefining the Status of Immigrants in Europe*, Aldershot: Avebury.

Bauböck, R., Heller, A. and Zolberg, A. R. (eds) (1996) *The Challenge of Diversity*, Aldershot: Avebury, European Center Vienna V. 21.

Brubaker, W. R. (ed.) (1989) *Immigration and the Politics of Citizenship in Europe and North America*, London: University Press of America.

Carens, J. H. (1987) 'Aliens and citizens: the case for open borders', *Review of Politics*, 49/2: 251–73.

Carens, J. H. (1989) 'Membership and morality: admission to citizenship in liberal democratic states', in Brubaker (ed.): 31–49.

Carens, J. H. (1995) 'Immigration, welfare, and justice', in Schwartz (ed.).

Carens, J. H. (1996) 'Realistic and Idealistic Approaches to the Ethics of Migration', *International Migration Review*, 30/1: 156–70.

Carens, J. H. (1997) 'Liberalism and culture', *Constellations*, 4/1: 35–47.

Cassese, A. (1993) *Los derechos humanos en el mundo contemporáneo*, Barcelona: Ariel.

Cesarani, D. and Fulbrook, M. (eds) (1996) *Citizenship, Nationality and Migration in Europe*, London: Routledge.

Dahl, R. (1992) *La democracia y sus críticos*, Barcelona: Paidós.

Dummet, A. and Nicol, A. (1990) *Subjects, Citizens, Aliens and Others: Nationality and Immigration Law*, London: Weidenfeld and Nicolson.

Edwards, G. and Wiessala, G. (eds) (1998) *The European Union 1997: Annual Review of Activities*, Oxford: Blackwell and Journal of Common Market Studies.

Elster, J. (1989) *The Cement of Society*, Cambridge: Cambridge University Press.

Geddes, A. (2000) *Immigration and European Integration: Towards Fortress Europe?*, Manchester: Manchester University Press.

Goodin, R. E. (1992) 'If people were money . . .', in Barry and Goodin (eds).

Habermas, J. (1992–3) 'Citizenship and national identity: some reflections on the future of Europe', *Praxis International*, 12: 1–19.

Habermas, J. (1999) *La inclusión del otro*, Madrid: Paidós.

Hailbronner, K. (1989) 'Citizenship and nationhood in Germany', in Brubaker (ed.).

Hammar, T. (1989) 'State, nation, and dual citizenship', in Brubaker (ed.).

Held, D. (1997) *Democracy and the Global Order*, Cambridge: Polity Press.

Hobsbawm, E. J. (1990) *Nations and Nationalism since 1780*, Cambridge: Cambridge University Press.

Hollifield, J. F. (1992) *Immigrants, Markets, and States*, Cambridge, Mass.: Harvard University Press.

Jacobson, D. (1996) *Rights across Borders: Immigration and the Decline of Citizenship*, London: Johns Hopkins University Press.

Kellas, J. G. (1991) *The Politics of Nationalism and Ethnicity*, London: MacMillan.

Kymlicka, W. (1989) 'Liberal individualism and liberal neutrality', *Ethics*, 99: 883–905.

Kymlicka, W. (1995) *Multicultural Citizenship*, Oxford: Clarendon Press.

Lapeyronnie, D. (ed.) (1992) *Immigrés en Europe: politiques locales d'intégration*, Paris: La Documentation Française.

Layton-Henry, Z. (ed.) (1990a) *The Political Rights of Migrant Workers in Western Europe*, London: Sage.

Layton-Henry, Z. (1990b) 'The challenge of political rights', in (ed.).

Layton-Henry, Z. (1990c) 'Citizenship or denizenship for migrant workers?', in (ed.).

Lehning, P. B. and Weale, A. (eds) (1997) *Citizenship, Democracy and Justice in the New Europe*, London: Routledge.

Lucas, J. de (1994) *El desafío de las fronteras*, Madrid: Temas de Hoy/Ensayo.

Miller, D. (1995) *On Nationality*, Oxford: Clarendon Press.

Miller, M. J. (1989) 'Political participation and representation of noncitizens', in Brubaker (ed.).

Nussbaum, M. C. and Cohen, J. (eds) (1996) *For Love of Country*, Boston, Mass.: Beacon Press.

Oomen, T. K. (1997) *Citizenship, Nationality, and Ethnicity*, Cambridge: Polity Press.

Parekh, B. (1991) 'British citizenship and cultural difference', in G. Andrews (ed.) *Citizenship*, London: Lawrence and Wishart.

Parekh, B. (1998) 'Integrating minorities in a multicultural society', in U. K. Preuß and F. Requejo (eds) *European Citizenship, Multiculturalism and the State*, Baden-Baden: Nomos.

Rath, J. (1990) 'Voting rights', in Layton-Henry (ed.).

Rex, J. (1996) *Ethnic Minorities in the Modern Nation State*, London: Macmillan.

Robertson, A. H. and Merrills, J. G. (1993) *Human Rights in Europe: A Study of the European Convention on Human Rights*, Manchester: Manchester University Press.

Schnapper, D. (1994) *La Communauté des citoyens: sur l'idée moderne de nation*, Paris: Gallimard.

Schwartz, W. F. (ed.) (1995) *Justice in Immigration*, Cambridge: Cambridge University Press.

Soysal, Y. N. (1994) *Limits of Citizenship: Migrants and Postnational Membership in Europe*, Chicago: The University of Chicago Press.

Tamir, Y. (1993) *Liberal Nationalism*, Princeton, NJ: Princeton University Press.

Ugur, M. (1998) 'Libertad de circulación versus exclusión: una reinterpretación de la división "propio-extraño" en la Unión Europea', in G. Malgesini (comp.) *Cruzando fronteras: migraciones en el sistema mundial*, Madrid: Icaria/Fundación Hogar del Empleado.

Valle, A. (1998) 'La refundación de la libre circulación de personas, Tercer pilar y Schengen: el espacio europeo de libertad, seguridad y justicia', *Revista de Derecho Comunitario*, 3: 41–78.

Waldron, J. (1992) 'Minority cultures and the cosmopolitan alternative', *University of Michigan Journal of Law Reform*, 25, 3/4: 751–93.

Walzer, M. (1982) 'Pluralism in political perspective', in M. Walzer *et al.* (eds) *The Politics of Ethnicity*, Cambridge, Mass.: Belknap Press of Harvard University Press.

Walzer, M. (1983) *Spheres of Justice: A Defense of Pluralism and Equality*, New York: Basic Books.

Walzer, M. (1993) 'Exclusion, injustice, and the democratic state', *Dissent*, 40: 55–64.

Walzer, M. (1997) *On Toleration*, New Haven, Conn.: Yale University Press.

Weiner, M. (1995) *The Global Migration Crisis: Challenge to States and to Human Rights*, New York: HarperCollins.

Weiner, M. (1996) 'Ethics, national sovereignty and the control of immigration', *International Migration Review*, 30/1: 171–97.

Wieviorka, M. (ed.) (1997) *Une société fragmentée?Le multiculturalisme en débat*, Paris: La Découverte.

Wieviorka, M. (1998) *Le racisme, une introduction*, Paris: La Découverte.

Young, I. M. (1989) 'Polity and group difference: a critique of the ideal of universal citizenship', *Ethics*, 99: 250–74.

Young, I. M. (1990) *Justice and the Politics of Difference*, Princeton, NJ: Princeton University Press.

Zapata, R. (1998a) 'Thinking European citizenship from the perspective of an eventual Euro-foreigner', in U. K. Preuß and F. Requejo (eds) *European Citizenship, Multiculturalism and the State*, Baden-Baden: Nomos.

Zapata, R. (1998b) 'Ciudadanía europea y extranjería', *Claves de la razón práctica*, 87: 29–35.

Zapata, R. (1998c) 'Ciudadanía europea y extranjería', *Claves de la razón práctica*, 87: 29–35.

Zapata, R. (1999) '¿Necesitamos un nuevo concepto de ciudadanía? Estabilidad democrática y pluralismo cultural', *Revista Internacional de Filosofía Política*, 13: 119–49.

Zapata, R. (2000a) *Ciudadanía, justicia y pluralismo cultural: hacia un nuevo contrato social* Barcelona: Anthropopos.

Zapata, R. (2000b) 'Justicia para extranjeros: mercado e inmigración', *Revista Española de Investigación Sociológica* , 90: 159–81.

Zapata, R. (2000c) 'Política de inmigración y Unión Europea', *Claves de la razón práctica*, 104: 26–32.

Zapata, R. (2000d) 'Nous reptes per a la teoria liberal-democràtica: justícia i immigració', *Diàlegs*, 3, 8: 31–55.

Zapata, R. (2000e) 'Inmigración e innovación política', *Revista Migraciones*, 8.

Zolo, D. (1997) *Cosmopolis: Prospect for World Government*, Cambridge: Polity Press.

# Part IV

# Pluralism, democracy and political theory

# 8  Democratic legitimacy and national pluralism

*Ferran Requejo*

> In political and philosophical theories as well as in persons, success dis-
> closes faults and infirmities which failure might have concealed from
> observation.
>
> (John Stuart Mill, *On Liberty*, 1859)

In this final chapter, I present some key issues of liberal-democratic
legitimacy in plurinational polities. The first section includes two
facets of political legitimacy based on the linguistic components of
present-day normative pluralism: the absence of one single theory or
conception of democratic legitimacy, and the relationship between
different narrative political languages and the construction of personal
and collective identities. The second and third sections focus, respectively, on the two most important general approaches within the
current discussion of democratic liberalism and on a revision of universalism and particularism, both in relation to plurinational polities.
Finally, taking into account the previous three sections, the fourth
section offers a review of some elements of Kantian philosophy as a
way to establish an updated liberal approach to political legitimacy
in plurinational democracies.

## Democratic legitimacy and normative pluralism

Few if any can be unaware of the increasingly descriptive and normative complex nature of the notions of 'pluralism' and 'progress' in the
liberal democracies at the beginning of the twenty-first century. On
the one hand, in the field of democratic legitimacy, there are an increasing number of plural legitimising values and criteria which are not used
to being fully harmonised within a single and coherent whole. On the
other hand, what has, in fact, become more plural is the very notion

of *progress* itself. No longer can it be reduced to conform to any of the ideologies that, as little as a few decades ago, claimed to hold the monopoly over the idea. This increase in the complexity of democratic pluralism and in the notion of progress has practical as well as theoretical consequences.

On the one hand, in the practical field, political decision-makers find themselves faced, now more than ever, with a plurality of often contradictory criteria – both of a technical and moral nature – and with a series of heterogeneous ambits in which policies are in themselves unequal or unable to be validly compared. Such decision-makers also find themselves with a context of the ever-changing social groups and political participants involved, with citizens who are increasingly well informed and who feel themselves more clearly linked to different historical, political and cultural collectives, and with differing perceptions of policies carried out or that ought to be carried out.

On the other hand, current political theory emphasises two facets of democratic legitimacy, namely the conviction that there is no political theory, not even political tradition, that may attribute such legitimacy exclusively to itself, and the recognition of the relationship that exists between different kinds of *narrative* political languages and the construction of personal and collective identities.[1]

These are two facets which have an effect on current democratic practice, having their epistemological reference point in the *linguistic turn* of contemporary philosophy, most especially that which starts with the pragmatic linguistics of Wittgenstein in *Philosophische Untersuchungen* (1951). In general terms, the philosophy of language in the first three decades of the twentieth century insisted that thinking about rationality effectively meant, in large part, thinking about language. In contrast with earlier periods of the 'philosophy of conscience', it is now maintained that there is no 'essence' to discover, but rather that there are linguistic 'objectivisations' of experience. A second stage to the linguistic focus on rationality, particularly from the time of Wittgenstein's revision of his earlier work (*Tractatus*) offers us a new *pragmatic turn*: the concept of *logical form* in language – which we never comprehend – gives way to the *rules* of *language games*, a differentiated group of uses and forms of life with which, as individuals, 'we open ourselves to the world'.[2] It is this latter period of the philosophy of language that is of particular relevance to the political sphere. Epistemologically, the emphasis is now on contextualisation and cognitive plurality. This, then, dilutes the idea of a single founding rationality, whether it be scientific or of a different nature. We could say that plurality and contextualisation explode within the very interior of the discourse of scientific disciplines: there is neither a single language, nor is there – in the languages existing – the same 'logical form'. Obviously, contextualising the different theoretical approximations, as well as underlining their plurality, does not imply the admittance of an epistemological or moral relativism of a 'postmodern' character, but rather, it questions the claims of the 'foundational uniqueness' in certain contemporary democratic theories.

The first facet, the absence of one single theory of democratic legitimacy, situates us within the democratic context of normative plurality. This is a question that has been analysed, among others, in history and linguistics studies by Q. Skinner and J. Pocock. Language always structures that which we wish to emphasise on the basis of certain rules situated beyond the simple wishes of the interlocutors (Skinner 1988, 1991; Pocock 1984, 1985). Understanding a political theory implies understanding the key outstanding questions, and the *speech acts* that are used in any given context (Searle 1995). Here we understand legitimising political languages more as context than as text. In this way, each of the great traditions of political theory – liberalism, socialism, republicanism, conservatism, cultural pluralism – in emphasising certain issues within the political sphere, use a whole series of specific conceptual and analytical tools that construct a given *narrative* on political relations, and propose given attitudes or solutions in order to provide answers to those issues that each theory has selected as being of greatest importance in the public arena. These include, for instance, individual liberty and the limitation of power; social equality and the criticism of capitalism; the development of civic virtue and legitimised links with the political community; political stability and social cohesion based on communal feelings, values and customs; or the recognition and promotion of differentiated identities considered as priorities for the individuals of any given group. Each one of those political traditions is informative, whether this be on an analytical or normative level, in relation to those questions raised by the various conceptions themselves, and in relation to their own 'nuclear' concepts; but at the same time, each one draws a *veil of silence* over a significant part of the areas emphasised by other political traditions. As a consequence, there is no single theory of democracy, at this stage in our history, that can claim to be an exclusive and exhaustive version of the legitimacy of such a form of government. Rather, we find ourselves faced with what are, in effect, partial theories that on the one hand underline, and simultaneously foster, specific aspects of democratic legitimacy; but on the other hand, detract from or even hide from view other aspects of this legitimacy when such aspects turn out to be alien to the 'rules' (Wittgenstein) of their particular narrative. It is not possible to establish a clear distinction between political thought and the language in which it is expressed (Pitkin 1972).

The second facet, the interrelation between narrative and identity, has also been emphasised in recent years by writers as disparate as R. Rorty (1989), M. Walzer (1987), Ch. Taylor (1989) or even H. Arendt (1993). The central point is the role of beliefs and values in the construction of modern identities through a narrative conception of identity, situated beyond the abstract and individualistic conceptions of a more formal character, which are usual in standard approaches to democratic liberalism (currently represented by, for example, J. Rawls and J. Habermas).[3] This interrelation concerns both the particular identities that define what we are (and which in large measure we do not choose), and the ways of theorising about such identities that modern times have given rise to (Mitchell 1980; Hinchman and Hinchman 1977; Newman 1966).

Narrative conforms to an inevitable and essential trait in human life. It is a trait which, on a normative level, emphasises the need to accommodate the 'ethical' dimension of practical rationality within the 'moral' rules of democracies.[4] In this way, the very sense of progress will be related to the theoretical narrations coming to us through the interrelation with others who always belong to specific groups, and that construct the referential frameworks from and within which we orientate ourselves, morally speaking, in an increasingly interrelated world. These frameworks are always unfinished, and always reveal their particular historical, dynamic and contextual character, however much their language might be filled with terms that aim to be semantically more definitive or 'universal'. In fact, theoretical revision and practical reformism form a part, as Protagoras very well understood, of the morally ever-perfectible character of democracy.

At the beginning of the twenty-first century, the analytical importance of the two facets of democratic legitimacy outlined above lies in the ability to evaluate more precisely both the different theories of political legitimacy, and their practical results. We know that the liberal tradition has been (and, we would add, fortunately so) the hegemonic tradition in this process of construction. But we also know that liberal democracies are historical 'products' that, in practice, have been constructed and conceived by the state. As I have said on other occasions, modern theories of democracy are, fundamentally, theories of the democratic *state*. The inherent '*statism*' of such theories is a characteristic that can hardly be 'neutral' when it comes to considering pluralism in the institutional concretion, or when proceeding to evaluate it on the basis of emancipatory terms suggested by contemporary political theories, and most especially by theories that are rooted in liberalism. It is this characteristic of liberal theories that we shall be examining in the following section in relation to plurinational societies.

## Liberal-democratic theories and national pluralism

One of the central points in current revisions of democratic liberalism within plurinational contexts, like Belgium, Canada, the United Kingdom or Spain, is based on the practical consequences that have been brought about by the 'statism', and its inherent nationalism, of empirical democracies. Here we usually find ourselves faced with a contrast between liberal theory and liberal practice. In fact, *in practice*, all liberal democracies have been nationalist realities. Nevertheless, in some of the *theoretical* liberal democratic conceptions of greater influence, the relationship between liberalism and nationalism has been presented as a relationship between irreconcilable positions. This is based on comprehending the two as representing general political positions that are founded on values, concepts and internal logic that are simply in contrast: any attempt to reconcile the two perspectives would be condemned to failure. Yet this is a notion that is becoming increasingly obsolete, particularly in contemporary circumstances presided over as they are by globalisation and national pluralism. In today's context, the debate is no longer between *democratic liberalism* on the one hand, and *nationalism* on the other, but rather it is between two basic and essential ways of understanding democratic liberalism and nationalism themselves or, if we prefer, between two different variants of democratic liberalism when it comes up against globalisation and cultural and national pluralism.[5]

In relation to 'the national question', the first variant defends a concept based, essentially, on individual rights of a 'universal' kind, on a 'non-discriminatory' idea of equality for all citizens, and on a series of procedural mechanisms that regulate institutional principles and the collective processes of decision-making. It is a form of political liberalism that distrusts the very notion of *collective rights*, suspecting such a concept of bringing authoritarian risks in its wake (*liberalism 1*). The second variant adds to these elements those of the protection and development, in the public and constitutional spheres, of specific cultural and political 'differences' for distinct national groups living within the same democracy. It holds that the absence of political and constitutional recognition and of broad-ranging self-government, results in a discriminatory bias against national minorities and in favour of national majorities, and that this thereby violates the principle of equality. Obviously, the possible conflicts that might arise between values and rights of a *collective* nature and those of an *individual* sort – a distinction that is often less than clear in reality – will have to be resolved through institutional mechanisms similar to those which resolve conflicts that arise in the area of individual rights themselves. According to this position, the first variant of political liberalism provides incentives to restricting minority national differences to the private sphere, all the while accepting the national cultural characteristics of the majority (language, history, traditions, etc.) as an implicit 'common' reality within the public sphere of the polity (*liberalism* 2).[6]

One of the questions that has been of particular weight in the normative and institutional debate between these two versions of political liberalism has been that of the *constitutional accommodation* for the different national collectives living together within the same democratic polity.[7] *Liberalism 2* has tended to emphasise the fact that the language, markedly universal, in favour of the individual rights of the citizens, of equality and of non-discrimination used by those in favour of *liberalism 1*, has – in practice – led to discrimination and marginalisation of national characteristics not coinciding with those of the majority or hegemonic national groups within the polity. For the minority nations, the price to pay for equality of citizenship often has been a situation of inequality in terms of linguistic and cultural personality in the public sphere. In other words, citizenship does not come at the same cultural price for each and every one of the different national groups within liberal democratic polities. According to this approach, rights, institutions and the procedural rules included in the *moral minims* aimed at by liberalism 1 have implied, in fact, the acceptance in practice of a whole series of *collective* and *particular* rights and values. These are certainly far removed from the *cultural neutrality* and *universal* language usually claimed by the state in defence of the supporters of this version of democratic liberalism.

If one of the traditional criticisms levelled at political liberalism – and made both from conservative and socialist positions – was that of the contrast between the ideas described in liberal theory, and what was actually carried out by those polities calling themselves 'liberal', then today such criticism broadens from purely *social or socio-economic* components to include the *cultural* components that are to be found in liberal democracies. In more philosophical terms, we could say that the narrative set out by liberalism 1 does not bear sufficiently in mind what exactly is implied by the *linguistic and pragmatic* dimensions referred to earlier in this discussion. And this, then, damages certain aspects of the emancipatory project laid out by this version of political liberalism.

On the other hand, what is demanded in plurinational contexts by liberalism 2 is, specifically, the possibility to realise more clearly the values of liberty, equality and individual dignity, which form the core part of contemporary liberalism's emancipatory project, by means of an effective accommodation of the different national realities living together within the same democracy. That is, in order to improve plurinational democracies in both an *ethical* and *moral* sense, there would have to be the inclusion, in the practical regulation of those abstract values, of the different national collective identities that go to making up the individuality of the citizens within one and the same polity. This is a question that is often concealed in the conception of a basic national public sphere assumed by liberalism 1, under culturally homogenising concepts such as national sovereignty, popular sovereignty or citizen equality.

I think that the step from liberalism 1 to liberalism 2 may presuppose a broadening of pluralism with the aim of including certain cultural dimensions that, up to now, have been undervalued or greatly marginalised in the liberal and democratic traditions of contemporary political thought. This is a broadening that, in fact, is facilitated by the very same 'universalist' language used by the narrative of the liberal tradition. It aims at widening the semantic content of certain liberal notions such as those of pluralism, equality or liberty, and – at the same time – at undermining the limitations and biases of its manifestations based on the *statism* and *nationalism* maintained in practice by liberal democracies. In other (and more 'postmodern') words, while liberalism 1 is well placed at the moment of accommodating the first of the two considerations on narration mentioned in the previous section: the non-existence of monopolies within languages as regards the democratic legitimacy of Western societies, liberalism 2 sets out the second consideration and, what is more, connects it to the first: the inevitably constructed character of any individual or collective identity. In this way, we could say that liberalism 1 tends to move with more ability in the area of *semantic* reflections, since these do not question the power relations within the linguistic context in which such reflections ought really to be situated, while liberalism 2 places itself within an area that is more fully the domain of linguistic *pragmatics*, since it questions the basic uniqueness and homogeneity of that context.

Understood from this point of view, the majority of claims made by minority democratic nationalisms (i.e. Catalan, Scottish, or Québécois) represent a deepening of the universal suppositions of political liberalism, and particularly of the values of equality, liberty and pluralism.[8] The key task is to understand that, in a plurinational democracy, a plural set of public spheres coexist, as well as different processes of nation-building.[9] In this way, the political and constitutional regulation of this specific kind of pluralism thus becomes a demand of liberal and federal legitimacy themselves at the beginning of the twenty-first century.[10]

In essence, then, the defence of national differences and its *politics of recognition* within the political sphere, presupposes a more precise version of a form of universalism capable of exercising a more open and critical role in relation to existing and globalised realities.[11] It is in this sense that I believe in the importance of a universalism that is not understood as a closed conquest, or as one which has been attained from values interpreted purely in the light of one type of narrative, but rather as a never-ending perspective that allows for the combating of the 'pathologies' which sometimes accompany various different types of (state and non-state) nationalism, and of other peculiarities, such as the much-vaunted cosmopolitanism of traditional liberalism. In reality, we always argue from the position of cultural inheritances that have facets of both a universal and particular kind, and which fashion the individual identities that, in large part, come to us pre-formed. Adopting a true 'cosmopolitan' position in a plurinational context would mean making the moral stance adopted an increasingly *general* one, and to do so not on the basis of 'tolerance', but rather of *respect* for the plurality of national hermeneutic frameworks of reference. In the next two sections, I offer a revision of the legitimising role of universalism and particularism in plurinational polities, also focusing on Kantian philosophy as a source for establishing that *general* legitimising perspective in contrast with what is offered by traditional liberal universalism.

## Universalism and particularism in plurinational democracies

In general terms, it is possible to state that the question of interculturality or cultural pluralism has posed a new agenda of issues for democratic debate that are no longer limited to the language of individual rights and notions of liberty, equality and pluralism in the same way as traditional political liberalism has developed these notions. Among the cultural biases that liberalism 1 displays, and which condition both the concretion of democratic values and the practical constitutional regulations in plurinational democracies, the following stand out:

1   The absence of a theory of *demos* in the theories of democracy, or the absence of a theory of demarcation (borders) in traditional political liberalism. These questions have never been resolved by the legitimising bases of the different theories of democratic liberalism. In plurinational democracies, the challenge to be addressed is 'one polity, several *demoi*', which implies a revision of the homogenising versions of some legitimising notions, such as of 'democratic citizenship' or 'popular sovereignty'.

2   The marginalisation, or even the non-existence, of the truly 'ethical' and contextual dimension of practical rationality within the theories of democratic legitimacy, in contrast to the position occupied by the 'instrumental' and 'moral' dimensions of this rationality in the different versions of these theories (utilitarian, Kantian or perfectionist). Liberal-democratic theories have tended to consider normative regulations from the perspective of instrumental and moral rationalities. The ethical considerations of a historical and linguistic nature, among others, that influence national identities have tended either to be marginalised or relegated to the private sphere (territorial minority national identities), or have simply been accepted implicitly as a kind of hermeneutic horizon of the public sphere (majority or hegemonic national identities). The political institutions have not been culturally neutral, but leaned towards the identities and cultural patterns of the national majority or hegemonic groups. A minimal conclusion is that from liberal premises there has been a tendency to accept and defend from the public sphere, an implicit form of state communitarianism of a 'national' nature.

3   The almost exclusive consideration of public sphere *justice* from the perspective of the *paradigm of equality* (equality versus inequality), in detriment to the *paradigm of difference* (equality versus difference). The juxtaposition of these two paradigms is fundamental in the context of cultural pluralism as in the case of plurinational societies (repercussions occur in different public spheres and policies such as cultural assimilation, political integration or politico-cultural accommodation).

4   The defence of nation-building in all liberal democracies: the homogenising cultural consequences of nation-building based on the

application of a universalist legitimising language to a particular group, the polity, that itself possesses a plurality of national groups.

The consideration of these aspects involves a revision of the role of normative universality in democratic legitimation and of its relation with values of a more particular nature in plurinational polities. A normative and institutional refinement of liberal democracies means seeing national pluralism as a value worth protecting and not just as an inconvenient fact that must be borne as stoically as possible. All liberal democracies have, in practice, defended and continue to defend cultural particularisms of a linguistic or historical nature.[12] This means that it is no longer pertinent to consider as mutually exclusive the contrast between a form of universalism based on egalitarian components of human 'dignity' and a form of particularism based on the cultural elements that individuals acquire through processes of socialisation. In a pluralist society, while universalist values are part of the identities of particular individuals, particular cultural values influence the concept of dignity itself. Therefore, the often accurate criticisms that liberal universalism has regularly directed at particularist positions, insofar as they lean towards conservatism and a lack of clear decision-making references, should be complemented with the no less accurate criticisms of culturally rooted particularism aimed at traditional universalism: lack of realism in relation to the normative links that individuals maintain with the groups and collectivities that they belong to and, above all, in relation to the practical inevitably of defending a set of specific cultural particularities in the name of this alleged universalism.[13]

On the other hand, the distinction between universalist and particularist normativities should itself be distinguished from the application of the two kinds of normativity. In the processes of democratic legitimation, neither does universality coincide with impartiality, nor particularity with partiality.[14] In other words, it is essential to bear in mind the distinction between an *impartial way* of putting into practice both a universalist normativity and a particularist normativity based on the uniform implementation of the norms and criteria for all the individuals and groups of the collective; and a *partial way* of carrying out this implementation by directing it at specific persons and groups that make up the collective. This latter type of implementation can be observed in policies of positive discrimination or affirmative action directed at different social groups according to their gender, social class, language, and so on, and may be of a *transitory* nature in order to achieve *equality* with the rest of the collective or of a *permanent* nature in order to protect and develop the cultural *differences* of the minority group in relation to the majority of the collective. Thus it is possible to establish the existence of four possible combinations between these two pairs of concepts. These combinations clarify the existing relationship among the different versions of political liberalism. Table 8.1 synthesises the relationship between the different types of legitimising normativity (universal or particular) and their ways of application (impartial or partial) in plurinational democracies.

Moral autonomy cannot be separated from empirical individual self-identity, where national components usually play a decisive role. In the case of plurinational democracies like Belgium, Canada, the United Kingdom or Spain, the perspective of liberalism 1, which is to *filter* those cultural particularisms that are incompatible with the universalism of 'loyalty to humanity' (Rorty 1997), must be complemented by the perspective of liberalism 2 in order to *departicularise* national statist biases that hegemonic cultural groups have imposed on all the citizens of the polity. In this way, plurinational democracies display plural forms of national identity that are basic for the different forms in which individual dignity and self-esteem are expressed.

These kinds of theoretical and practical revisions will have consequences for political philosophy. If not only 'morality', but also the *ethicities* are relevant for the political legitimacy of plurinational democracies, we may say that this favours the flexibilisation of the Kantian perspective, as it has been traditionally interpreted, towards a more Humean or Hegelian attitude.[15] However, I believe that Kant's work offers more sensitive interpretations for the pluralism of national identities, above all when one questions the implicit liberal statism that dominates the 'constructivist' and 'reconstructivist' versions of Kantism in current theories about the legitimacy of political association, such as those of Rawls (1993, 1995) or Habermas (1994, 1996a).[16]

## Legitimacy and national pluralism: a Kantian approach

In previous works, I considered the relative failures of Rawls and Habermas to establish liberal-democratic foundations for plurinational polities (Requejo 1998a, 2000). These failures are based on the limitations of the intellectual traditions from which they stem. Both theories display the same *statist* perspective which selects and impoverishes the kinds of pluralism under consideration and which, more crucially,

Table 8.1 Types of legitimising normativity and ways of applying it

| | Type of legitimising normativity in plurinational democracies | | |
| --- | --- | --- | --- |
| | **Universalist normativity**<br>*Legitimation based on values and interests linked to the 'dignity' of any human being in the polity* | **Particularist normativity**<br>*Legitimation based on values and interests linked to the cultural 'differences' of collectives or specific groups in the polity* | |
| **Ways of applying the normativity** | | National (territorial) collectivities | Cultural groups |
| **Impartial**<br>*Uniform application of rules and criteria to all individuals and groups* | Legitimation of individual 'human rights' of a civic participatory, socio-economic and cultural nature in a specific polity (Kantian, perfectionist and utilitarian theories)<br><br>(Liberalism 1) | National (territorial) collectivities: political recognition plus national self-governments (states, minority national collectivities)<br>Legitimation of specific rights and values (individual and collective), regulation of political institutions and internal policies of the national collectivities<br><br>(Liberalism 2) | Cultural groups (without territoriality) (immigrants, religious, etc.)<br>Legitimation of specific rights and values<br><br>(Liberalism 1 and 2) |
| **Partial**<br>*Application of rules and criteria in favour of specific individuals and groups* | Legitimation of internal policies of positive discrimination (gender, social class, language, etc.) | | |
| | (Transitory policies) | (Permanent policies) | |

avoids dealing with the contentious issue of the pre-eminence of the particularism of a state *demos*, while turning a blind eye to any internal national pluralism. The contractualism of these theories fails to question who should be the subjects of the contract. They establish a number of 'moral points of view' that are loaded with state *ethicity* that is unjustifiable from the 'liberal' premises of the theories themselves.

A possible alternative route to establish a form of liberalism that is sensitive to the pluralism of different national identities consists in recovering the link between liberty and rationality which is developed in Kant's critical approach. Paradoxical though it may seem, it may be possible to say that, despite Rawls' and Habermas' references to Kant's work,[17] the latter may provide a good alternative route to the limits of the former two, if it is conceived in more Hegelian terms than is normally the case.[18] This is possible with reference not only to the 'historical writings' of his last period, but also to the notion of regulative idea, developed in the transcendental dialectics of the first critique, and to liberty as a postulate for practical reason.[19]

When one is attempting to regulate a conception of human 'dignity', which also includes the perspective of 'differences' of identity, it is my view that the potential of the ideas of theoretical reason and liberty as a proposition for practical reason in the sphere of liberal political philosophy has not been sufficiently explored. My proposal consists of considering the recognition of dignity and national identity differences as ideas of Kantian reason. The potential of both concepts for plurinational democracies can be visualised in two steps. The first step is to remember that the problems posed by Kantian reason cannot be unequivocally resolved (antimonies, paralogisms), nor can they be rejected (KRV, AV11).[20] The ideas of reason are not 'invented' problems (KRV, B386), but the basis of questions that we are unable to answer with certainty, and which it is not 'rational' to abandon for supposedly rigourous positions. These ideas are not knowledge, nor can they be knowledge. They are not measured in 'categories' because reason (*Vernunft*) does not constitute, but orders (B 671), regulates (B 672) and globalises (B 814, B 730). Therefore, unlike understanding (*Verstand*) which refers to data, reason is discursive (B 359).[21] This is a theoretical framework that allows one to escape from the tendency displayed by liberal political philosophy to approach democratic legitimacy in terms of 'understanding' and to overly separate the descriptive and normative levels as far as the consideration of democratic institutional practices is concerned. Anticipating the considerations of later philosophers, Kant established that the unity of reason presupposes that the whole precedes the individual parts (KRV 673). Despite not referring to objectivity as sensitivity or understanding (B670), reason not only works 'at dusk', or in other words, *after* understanding, but also precedes, regulates and directs it (B708). In this way, as far as the consideration of dignity and recognition of national differences of identity are concerned, universality should make way for 'generality': reason is not a cognitive skill, but a thinking skill. His ideas 'show' (Wittgenstein), the ideal of finding principles and laws that are increasingly *general* for the refinement of the normative and narrative perspectives of plurinational democracies.

The second step in Kant's reformulation of the normative bases of liberal democracies in plurinational contexts involves observing that Kant's reasoning regulates not objects, but subjectivity. And in this subjectivity, political liberty can also be understood as a process and a developmental framework for the ethical identities of the collectives, of the national *demos* that have yet to be regulated constitutionally. Political mediation does not occur between subjectivities and an abstract universality, but between the former and a series of generalities which are legitimised in universalist and particular terms. The key concept (or proposition) is liberty. Something which, in Kantian terms, must be understood to be undemonstrable, but which constitutes an assumption of morality itself. From this perspective it is easier to include the 'ethical' dimension inherent in national pluralism in the rules and institutions of 'justice' of the liberal tradition. The incorporation of *ethicity* in these rules and institutions gives them greater reflexivity to regulate individual and collective constitutional rights, by adapting them to specific contexts.[22] In the case of plurinational realities, this means articulating the political liberty of the different *demoi* within the 'moral' rules of liberal democracies. In other words, it means constitutionalising a concept of *complex political liberty* that includes individual and collective perspectives of the instrumental, ethical and moral dimensions of practical rationality.[23] These dimensions may enter into conflict, in the same way as individual rights do. It is not a question of ignoring these conflicts, but of institutionalising the constitutional mechanisms to resolve them.

If dignity and the recognition of differences of identity as ideas of reason favour the insertion of the liberal-democratic rules of the game in a number of general rather than universal principles, a complex form of political liberty as a proposition for practical reason favours an increasingly 'better' articulation between the ethical and moral dimensions of practical rationality in these rules. A theoretical attitude based on general principles and on the articulation of ethical and moral regulations within constitutional rules situates us before the perspective of a constant reformism on the road to achieving 'better' regulations for liberal-democratic normativity itself.

Modern democracy established that dissent is not incompatible with the progress and stability of a political collectivity. What has to be done now, from the perspective of a liberal politics of recognition for national identities is, on the one hand, pluralise the notion of pluralism as it is put into practice by the first liberal conceptions of modern democracy and, on the other hand, to break the *cultural and national monism* adopted by state nationalisms in their conception of the democratic *demos*.[24] In plurinational contexts, dissent is necessary to emancipate the individual from identities that are alien (or less close) to him or her and to refine individual liberty in the institutional sphere of liberal democracies.

In this way, Kantian philosophy allows the pluralism of national identities to be regarded as a value worth protecting, and not as a simple fact that has to be lived with. Normative and institutional progress towards 'democratically advanced societies' involves,[25] in the case of plurinational societies, a better constitutional accommodation of the historical and territorial national identities that exist in the polity.[26]

## Acknowledgements

I would like to thank Klaus-Jürgen Nagel, Sven Wynants and the other members of the *Grup de Teoria Política* in the Universitat Pompeu Fabra (Barcelona), for their comments on draft versions of this chapter.

## Notes

1 This relationship seems to be independent of the fact that such languages hold within them concepts of a more universal or more particular vocation. The term 'identity' refers here both to the characteristics that singularise an individual or a group in relation to other individuals or groups, as well as to 'auto-referential' (narrative) characteristics established by both types of entity.

2 See a 'sample' – in the statistical sense – of the *pragmatic turn* (Wittgenstein) in the comparison of the following passages (T: *Tractatus*, PU: *Philosophische Untersuchungen*): T 4.021, 4.022, 4.023 – PU 23, 24, 291, 610 ; T 4.024 – PU 199, XI2p; T 4.03 – PU 105, 107, 116; T 5.5563 – PU 97, 102; T 6.412, 6.13 – PU 77; T 651 – PU 84, 85, 87; T 6.53, 6.54, 7 – PU 109, 122, 123, 125, 128, 133, 309.

3 An analysis of the deficiencies encountered in the conceptions offered by Rawls and by Habermas when confronting plurinational polities can be found in Requejo 1998a; 2000.

4 The dimension of practical rationality that is most strictly *ethical*, associated with the contexts of particular societies, and in which both the specific narrative of national cultures and the will for group continuity play a vital role, has generally been marginalised by the conceptions of democratic liberalism in favour of the *pragmatic* and *moral* dimensions of this rationality.

5 For the relationship between democratic liberalism and nationalism, see Requejo 1999c, McKim and McMahan 1997, Caney et al. 1996, Canovan 1996, Norman 1996, Miller 1995, Smith 1995, Yack 1995, Tamir 1993, Nodia 1992. See also the different stages in the discussion over minority rights pointed out by Kymlicka's Chapter 2 in this volume.

6 I maintain here the terms liberalism 1 and 2, following the well-known expression formulated by Ch. Taylor and M. Walzer. It is certainly not without significance that, in plurinational polities, the supporters of *liberalism 1* are the majority in Ottawa, Toronto, London or Madrid; whereas the supporters of *liberalism 2* are more likely to be found in cities such as Montreal, Edinburgh or Barcelona.

7 This accommodation includes two basic dimensions of the national plurality of a state: explicit *recognition* of its internal national plurality, also at a constitutional level, and the rules that regulate the *democratic self-government* of those groups. See Tully 1994. For a broader discussion of multiculturalism and liberal democracy, see also Requejo 1999a, M. Williams 1995, Kymlicka 1995, Spinner 1994, Raz 1994, Parekh 1993. For a panoramic analysis of the concept of democratic citizenship within the ambit of political theory, see Norman and Kymlicka 1994. See also Wilmsen and McAllister 1996; Elósegui 1998, Avnon and de Shalit 1999, Cordell 1999. In relation to constitutional issues related to plurinationality, see Norman's discussion on the convenience of including a right of political secession in democratic constitutions, and Fossas' approach to equality in plurinational societies, Chapters 5 and 4 respectively in this volume.

8 See Keating's analysis (Chapter 3 in this book) for an approach in a similar vein on current minority democratic nationalisms.

9 This is an idea that affects current discussion of whether federalism, or one of its variants, offers an adequate framework from which to proceed to a practical and constitutional accommodation for plurinational polities in which diverse processes of nation-building share the same arena. See Requejo 1998b, 1999b, Gibbins and Laforest 1998, McRoberts 1997. For a broader view of the debate surrounding asymmetrical federalism and its political and constitutional possibilities within plurinational states, see Fossas and Requejo 1999.

10 I have therefore proposed a model of *plural federalism* as being more suitable to accommodate national plurality. Three kinds of regulations are included in this model: an explicit constitutional recognition of the plurinationality of the federation; the asymmetrical or confederal regulation of the key powers for the self-government of national minori-

ties; and the symmetrical regulation of the rest of the powers. See Requejo 1999b, 2001.

11 An analysis of democracies and globalisation is in Resnick 1997, Axtmann 1996, Archibugi and Held 1995.

12 A criticism, for instance, of colonial and imperialist legitimation in the writings of Locke and Mill, in Parekh 1995.

13 See the debate between what we may refer to as 'liberal interculturalism' (B. Parekh) and 'intercultural liberalism' (W. Kymlicka), in *Constellations*, 4, 1 April 1997.

14 See Nagel 1996b; Miller 1995: ch. 3; Stocker 1992; Parfit 1984: III.

15 The Humean vindication of morality versus the universality of Kantism has been pointed out by B. Williams 1985. See also Tamir 1993: ch. 5.

16 McCarthy 1994. See also Klosko 1997.

17 Habermas has referred to his position as 'Kantian republicanism' (Habermas 1996b).

18 Hegel described the state as 'the effectiveness of the ethical idea' (Wirklichkeit der sittlichen Idee', 1257 RPh). The three components of the definition refer to the notions of truly implement (*werken*), to carry out a concept (*Idee*) in a suitable way, and belonging to public customs (*sittlichen*). This is a 'technical' definition within Hegel's work that we may 'translate' considering the state as that institution that permits the practical expression of rationality in human relations. The isolated man/woman of contractualist conceptions is a non-existent abstraction. In the real world, humans are always members of a particular society. (Civil) societies that left to their own 'selfish' devices would bring about the dissolution of *ethicity* itself. It is the state which permits the reconciliation between subjectivity and generality. From this perspective, a form of practical rationality that has fewer constitutional structures would also result in a state with less liberty. The very complexity of the three dimensions of practical rationality, whose implementation demands the existence of the state, means that it is never fully realised. However, the refinement or normative 'progress' of democratic states towards greater optimisation between the three dimensions of rationality implies the need to articulate plural *ethicities* that coexist within it and which have traditionally been marginalised. The incorporation of the particular 'ethical' dimensions in the regulation of a politics of recognition represents a step forward in the refinement of the 'moral' rules of constitutional liberal-democratic states.

19 The 'ideas of reason' of the first critique (KRV) *show*, although they cannot *say* (Wittgenstein), the ideal of finding ever more general laws and principles. The propositions of practical reason (among them, liberty), developed in the second critique (KPV), are necessary but undemonstrable requirements of morality. It is a single reason with two uses based on their own interests (B 715, B 826).

20 Metaphysics, condemned by positivist attitudes, is understood here in terms of disposition (KRV, AXI). (The references come from *The Critique of Pure Reason*.) See Kant's famous passage on the distinction between 'understanding' (scientific truths) as an island and 'reason' (metaphysics) as the ocean that surrounds it (KRV B295). I have developed this point from a critical perspective in relation to the work of Habermas, in Requejo 1991: ch. 2.

21 Later critics have pointed out that the dimension that seems to vanish in Kant's approach is that of historicity. The habitual lack of historical considerations in liberal theories that are based on the perspective of 'dignity' (liberalism 1) corresponds to the blurring of historicity in Kant's work. This was strongly criticised by the Frankfurt School (Horkheimer, Adorno). I believe that the Kantian dialectic is more fruitful if it is read in the context of Kant's own historical writings, which are closer to the attitudes of Aristotelian ethics and to Wittgenstein's linguistic pragmatics, and more favourable to the establishment of *general criteria* than to *universal principles* in the political sphere. This in turn favours a discrimination between the recognition of the differences of cultural identity of a historical and territorial nature (non-state nationalisms, indigenous collectives) and those without this characteristic (immigrant groups). I do not develop this point any further here. See Requejo 1999a.

22 In plurinational states one may see some of the 'ethical' consequences of the 'original dispositions' of unsociable human sociability. This is reflected in politicians' attitudes and in their use of language. Constitutional rights do not end at understanding; they are also to be found in the contextual and ethical relations between understanding and reason.

23 This concept is similar to the regulation of 'external protections' suggested by Kymlicka 1995.

24 'Pluralising pluralism' will involve three things: the incorporatation of marginalised national realities into the constitutional rights and rules; the consideration of national pluralism as valuable and not simply as a fact, and the establishment of practical solutions that take into account the individuals that make up that plurality.

25 The expression 'establish a democratically advanced society' appears in the introduction to the present Spanish constitution (1978) next to clearly statist references to a single, sovereign and indivisible Spanish state (Art. 1, 2).

26 I have developed this point in Requejo 2001.

# References

Archibugi, D. and Held, D. (1995), *Cosmopolitan Democracy*, Cambridge, Polity Press.

Arendt, H. (1993), *Between Past and Future*, Middlesex, Penguin.

Avnon, D. and de Shalit, A. (eds) (1999), *Liberalism and its Practice*, London, Routledge.

Axtmann, R. (1996), *Liberal Democracy into the Twenty-first Century*, Manchester, Manchester University Press.

Caney, S., George, D. and Jones, P. (eds) (1996), *National Rights, International Obligations*, Boulder, Col., Westview Press.

Canovan, M. (1996), *Nationhood and Political Theory*, Cheltenham, Elgar.

Cordell, K. (ed.) (1999), *Ethnicity and Democratization in the New Europe*, London, Routledge.

Elósegui, M. (1998), *El derecho a la igualdad y a la diferencia*, Madrid, Ministerio de Trabajo y Asuntos Sociales.

Fossas, E. and Requejo, F. (eds) (1999), *Asimetría Federal y Estado Pluri-nacional: El debate sobre la acomodación de la diversidad en Canadá, Bélgica y España*, Madrid, Trotta.

Gibbins J. and Laforest, G. (eds) (1998), *Beyond the Impasse*, Montreal, Institute for Research in Public Policy.

Habermas, J. (1994), 'Struggles for Recognition in the Democratic Constitutional State', in Ch. Taylor, *Multiculturalism: Examining the Politics of Recognition*, Princeton, NJ, Princeton University Press.

Habermas, J. (1996a), *Faktizität und Geltung*, Frankfurt, Suhrkamp.

Habermas, J. (1996b), 'Vernünftig versus "Wahr" oder die Moral der Weltbilder', *Einbeziehung des Anderen*, Frankfurt, Suhrkamp.

Hinchman, L. and Hinchman, S. (eds) (1997), *Memory, Identity, Community: The Idea of Narrative in the Human Sciences*, Albany, NY, SUNY Press.

Klosko, G. (1997), 'Political Constructivism in Rawls' Political Liberalism', *American Political Science Review*, 91, 3: 635–46.

Kymlicka, K. (1995), *Multicultural Citizenship: A Liberal Theory of Minority Rights*, Oxford, Clarendon Press.

McCarthy, T. (1994), 'Kantian Constructivism and Reconstructivism: Rawls and Habermas', in *Ethics*, 105: 44–63.

McKim, R. and McMahan, J. (eds) (1997), *The Morality of Nationalism*, Oxford, Oxford University Press.

McRoberts, K. (1997), *Misconceiving Canada: The Struggle for National Unity*, Toronto, Oxford University Press.

Miller, D. (1995), *On Nationality*, Oxford, Clarendon Press.

Mitchell, W. J. T. (ed.) (1980), *On Narrative*, Chicago, University of Chicago Press.

Nagel, T. (1996), *Equality and Partiality*, New York, Oxford University Press.

Newman, R. (ed.) (1966), *Centuries' Ends, Narrative Means*, Stanford, Calif., Stanford University Press.

Nodia, G. (1992), 'National and Democracy', *Journal of Democracy*, Baltimore, Md, Johns Hopkins University Press, 3, 4: 3–22.

Norman, N. and Kymlicka, K. (1994), 'Return of the Citizen: A Survey of Recent Work on Citizenship Theory', *Ethics* 104: 352–81.

Norman, W. (1996), 'The Ideology of Shared Values: A Myopic Vision of Unity in the Multi-Nation State', in J. Carens (ed.) *Is Quebec Nationalism Just? Perspectives from Anglophone Canada*, Montreal, McGill-Queen's University Press.

Parekh, B. (1993), 'The Cultural Particularity of Liberal Democracy', in D. Held (ed.) *Prospects for Democracy*, Cambridge, Polity Press.

Parekh, B. (1995), 'Liberalism and Colonialism: A Critique of Locke and Mill', in J. P. Nederveen Pieterse and B. Parekh (eds) *The Decolonization of Imagination*, London, Zed Books.

Parfit, D. (1984), *Reasons and Persons*, Oxford, Clarendon Press.

Pitkin, H. (1972), *Wittgenstein and Justice. On Significance of Ludwig Wittgenstein for Social and Political Thought*, Berkeley and Los Angeles, University of California Press.

Pocock, J. G. A. (1984), 'Verbalising a Political Act', in M. Shapiro (ed.) *Language and Politics*, Oxford, Basil Blackwell.

Pocock, J. G. A. (1985), *Virtue, Commerce and History*, Cambridge, Cambridge University Press.

Rawls, J. (1993), *Political Liberalism*, New York, Columbia University Press.

Rawls, J. (1995), 'Reply to Habermas', *Journal of Philosophy*, 92, 3: 132–80.

Raz, J. (1994), 'Multiculturalism: A Liberal Perspective', *Dissent*, Winter: 67–79.

Requejo, F. (1991), *Teoría Crítica y Estado Social: Neokantismo y Social-democracia en Jürgen Habermas*, Barcelona, Anthropos.

Requejo, F. (1998a), 'European Citizenship in Plurinational States. Some Limits of Traditional Democratic Theories: Rawls and Habermas', in U. Preuss and F. Requejo (eds) *European Citizenship, Multiculturalism and the State*, Baden-Baden, Nomos.

Requejo, F. (1998b), *Federalisme, per a què? L'acomodació de la diversitat en democràcies plurinacionals*, València, Tres i Quatre.

Requejo, F. (1999a), 'Cultural Pluralism, Nationalism and Federalism: A Revision of Citizenship in Plurinational States', *European Journal of Political Research*, 35, 2: 255–86.

Requejo, F. (1999b), 'La acomodación "federal" de la plurinacionalidad. Democracia liberal y Federalismo Plural en España', in Fossas and Requejo 1999.

Requejo, F. (1999c), *Pluralisme nacional y legitimitat democràtica*, Barcelona, Proa.

Requejo, F. (2000), 'El liberalismo político en estados plurinacionales: Rawls y Habermas y la legitimidad del federalismo plural', in Jean-François Prud'homme (comp.) *Demócratas, Liberales y Republicanos*, Mexico City, El Colegio de México.

Requejo, F. (2001), 'Political Liberalism in Plurinational States. The Legitimacy of Plural and Asymmetrical Federalism: The Case of Spain', in A. Gagnon and J. Tully (eds) *In Search of Justice and Stability: A Comparative and Theoretical Analysis of Canada, Belgium, Spain and the United Kingdom*, Cambridge, Cambridge University Press.

Resnick, P. (1997), *Twenty-first Century Democracy*, Montreal, McGill-Queen's University Press.

Rorty, R. (1989), *Contingency, Irony and Solidarity*, Cambridge, Cambridge University Press.

Rorty, R. (1997) 'Justice as a larger loyalty', in R. Bontekoe and M. Stepaniants (comps) *Justice and Democracy: Cross-Cultural Perspectives*, Honolulu: University of Hawaï Press.

Searle, J. (1995), *The Construction of Social Reality*, New York, Free Press.

Skinner, Q. (1988), 'Language and Social Change', in J. Tully (ed.) *Meaning and Context*, Princeton, NJ, Princeton University Press.

Skinner, Q (1991), 'Who are "we" ? Ambiguities of the Modern Self', *Inquiry*, 34, 2: 133–53.

Smith, A. (1995), *Nations and Nationalisms in a Global Era*, Cambridge, Polity Press.

Spinner, J. (1994), *The Boundaries of Citizenship: Race, Ethnicity and Nationality in the Liberal State*, Baltimore, Md, Johns Hopkins University Press.

Stocker, L. (1992), 'Interest and Ethics in Politics', *American Political Science Review*, 86: 369–80.

Tamir, Y. (1993), *Liberal Nationalism*, Princeton, NJ, Princeton University Press.

Taylor, Ch. (1989), *Sources of the Self: The Making of Modern Identity*, Cambridge, Cambridge University Press.

Taylor, Ch. (1992), 'The Politics of Recognition', in Amy Gutman (ed.) *Multiculturalism and the 'Politics of Recognition'*, Princeton, NJ, Princeton University Press.

Tully, T. (1994), *Strange Multiplicity: Constitutionalism in an Age of Diversity*, Cambridge, Cambridge University Press.

Walzer, M. (1987), *Interpretation and Social Criticism*, Cambridge, Mass., Harvard University Press.

Williams, B. (1985), *Ethics and the Limits of Philosophy*, Cambridge, Mass., Harvard University Press.

Williams, M. (1995), 'Justice toward Groups', *Political Theory*, 23, 1: 67–91.

Wilmsen, E. and McAllister, P. (eds) (1996), *The Politics of Difference*, Chicago, University of Chicago Press.

Yack, B. (1995), 'Reconciling Liberalism and Nationalism', *Political Theory*, 23, 1: 166–82.

# Index